# BLUE RIBBON
# CAKES & PIES

1-2-3-4 Butter Cake, page 132

# BLUE RIBBON
# CAKES & PIES

**NOTICE**

Mention of specific companies in this book does not imply endorsement by the publisher, nor does mention of specific companies imply that they endorse this book. Internet addresses and telephone numbers given in this book were accurate at the time it went to press.

© 2005 by Rodale Inc.

All rights reserved. No part of this publication may be reproduced or transmitted in any form or by any means, electronic or mechanical, including photocopying, recording, or any other information storage and retrieval system, without the written permission of the publisher.

Printed in the United States of America
Rodale Inc. makes every effort to use acid-free ⊗, recycled paper ♺.

*Cover photograph:* Mitch Mandel
*Cover recipe:* Red Velvet Cake
Courtesy of Tone Brothers, Inc., page 42
*Food stylist:* Dianne Vezza
*Illustrations:* Judy Newhouse

Editorial Produced by:
BETH ALLEN ASSOCIATES, INC.

*President/Owner:* Beth Allen
*Culinary Consultant/Food Editor:* Deborah Mintcheff
*Project Editors:* Stephanie Avidon, Melissa Moritz
*Nutritionist:* Michele C. Fisher, Ph.D., R.D.
*Recipe Editor:* Carol Prager
*Art Production Director:* Laura Smyth (smythtype)
*Photo Researcher:* Valerie Vogel

**Library of Congress Cataloging-in-Publication Data**

Blue ribbon cakes & pies
      p.   cm.
  Includes index.
  ISBN-13 978–1–59486–145–1 hardcover
  ISBN-10 1–59486–145–5 hardcover
  1. Cake.  2. Pies.  I. Rodale (Firm)
TX771.B57   2005
641.8'653—dc22      2004023633

2  4  6  8  10  9  7  5  3  1  hardcover

**We inspire and enable people to improve their lives and the world around them**
For more of our products visit **rodalestore.com** or call 800-848-4735

# CONTENTS

**INTRODUCTION  6**
*Meet me at the Fair*

**BLUE RIBBON BAKING  9**

**EVERYDAY CAKES & PIES  17**
*Cobbler, crisps, and snackin' cakes*

**LOTS OF CHOCOLATE  41**
*From pudding cakes to towering chocolate classics*

**FOR THE KIDS  65**
*It's Happy Birthday time!*

**FOR THE SEASON  83**
*Sweets, to match the season*

**CELEBRATIONS!  103**
*It's a special day, so bake a cake!*

**FOR THE CROWD  125**
*Plenty of pieces for all, and seconds too*

**CREDITS  140**

**WEB SITES  141**

**INDEX  142**

# INTRODUCTION

*Meet me at the fair and bring your favorite cake!*

The state fair starts tomorrow, so let's meet there—and don't forget that delicious triple layer fudge cake . . . it just might win a blue ribbon! You know the spot: Once you enter the fairgrounds, pass the food tents and head straight for the cake exhibition tent. The judging starts early, so don't be late!

If you're lucky enough to have attended—or better yet to have entered—a competition in a county or state fair, you know how exciting the day is. In fact, fairs really haven't changed all that much since the very first state fair in 1841 in Syracuse, New York—they've just gotten bigger and better! There's always so much going on. Check out the "classes" first (that's fair-lingo for the food judgings), with the luscious towering cakes, "mile-high" homemade pies, jars upon jars of every vegetable imaginable, fabulous fresh fruit jams and jellies, as well as pickled anything and everything.

But it doesn't stop there! You can visit exhibitions on every phase of country life—from quilts and hog-calling contests to cattle, quarter horse, and pig competitions. Enjoy an icy glass of freshly squeezed lemonade, stop in at a bluegrass concert, and join an old-fashioned taffy pull. Then, end the day with a juicy steak dinner at the cattlemen's pavilion. Once home, pick your favorite recipe from this *Blue Ribbon Cakes & Pies* collection, and treat your family and friends to your own winning dessert.

You're in for a surprise! You don't have to spend all day in the kitchen making these blue ribbon specials. Some take longer than others, of course, but they all use time-saving ingredients and techniques, such as prepared piecrust (or you can make your own!), speedy appliances to mix and chop quickly, and shortcuts to get these blue ribbon winners in and out of the kitchen fast.

Who can resist a wedge of Berry Sour Cream Shortcake (page 20) laden with fresh peaches and raspberries and smothered with freshly whipped cream? Or a slice of double-layered Red Velvet Cake (page 42) with rich Buttercream Frosting that tastes just like Grandma's (the one that won her a blue ribbon in 19 state fairs)? This one tastes the same, except Grandma took all day to make hers and this takes merely an hour. And if you're in a hurry, the Quick & Easy Fruit Cobbler can be prepared very fast. It's in and out of the oven in less than 30 minutes (look for the *SuperQuick* icon to find all of the other fast recipes).

Thumb through the pages and you'll find more cakes and pies that bring home blue ribbons year after year. Like the classic Buttery Pound Cake (page 22), the 3-Layer German Sweet Chocolate Cake (page 49) that's "just like Mom's" with its classic coconut-pecan icing, and the Blue Ribbon Apple Pie (page 92) with its cinnamon-spiced crust. You'll find new takes on familiar favorites such as a White Chocolate Coconut Cream Pie (page 55) and Red, White & Blue Cheesecake (page 109)—perfect for July Fourth celebrations.

As in the other books in The Quick Cook series, food professionals, cooking pros, and the test kitchens of well-known food manufacturers across the country bring generations of classic *Blue Ribbon Cakes & Pies*—and all of those memories served with them. Naturally, they'll be blue ribbon perfect every time, as they've all been tested and retested to guarantee desserts you'll be proud to serve.

In keeping with the other books in The Quick Cook series, *Blue Ribbon Cakes & Pies* is much more than just another recipe book. If your pound cake doesn't come out perfectly, check out the *Baking Basics* feature on "Butter Cake Fix-It Tips" on page 133. If your chocolate pie filling is thick and perfect when you put it into the shell but turns to "chocolate soup" later, find out why that happens and how to prevent it from happening again in the *Cook to Cook* conversation on page 51. There are other secrets that blue ribbon cooks know, such as how to store that last slice of leftover cake so that it's as fresh as the first (page 30).

There's more blue ribbon advice tucked inside, too. Look at the *Microwave in Minutes* feature on page 52 and find out how your microwave can help you melt chocolate in a flash. There are several fast crumb crusts you can make in minutes in your food processor (page 14) and even some ways to ice a cake fast (see *Baking Basics* on page 123). And for those evenings when you just want to curl up with a book, reach for this one and browse the *Food Facts*, including the one about how birthday cakes came to be (page 69).

While you're enjoying *Blue Ribbon Cakes & Pies*, don't forget that other great-tasting recipes and time-saving tips will be coming your way in future books in The Quick Cook collection. They, too, will be chock full with 100 fabulous recipes, beautiful photographs, and lots of useful quick-cooking tips.

But now's your chance to begin discovering what cooks have taken generations to learn: how to make every cake and pie you bake blue ribbon perfect. Even if you've never entered a state or county fair contest before, you'll immediately become a Blue Ribbon Baker!

*Blue Ribbon Apple Pie*, page 92

# Blue Ribbon Baking

Ask anyone who has ever won a blue ribbon at a fair for a baked good and they're likely to say that it took lots of work, but that it's worth it! First pick out the freshest ingredients—only the best should be used. Then head right home and start baking one of our blue ribbon recipes. Turn on the oven and measure carefully before mixing. If you're baking a cake, gently spoon the batter into the pans. If you're making a pie, flute the crust carefully and decorate the top. The look is almost as important as the way the pie slices and tastes. Now add the finishing touches and take the cake or pie to the fair—or to your table. You're on your way to becoming a winning baker!

*Gone to Heaven Chocolate Pie, page 51*

*Ice Cream Cake Roll, page 27*

*Choco-holic Cake, page 43*

## THE MAKINGS OF A BLUE RIBBON CAKE

What does it take to bring home a ribbon? State fair winners will tell you "the cake has to not only look good enough to eat but taste homemade, heavenly, and delicious as well." There's no one formula that guarantees a cake will be worthy of a ribbon (at the fair or with your friends), but here are some secrets that will help make everything you bake be of the highest quality with a great homemade touch and taste.

- **LAYER CAKES:** In order for a cake to be light and tender, you must start with a creamy—almost fluffy—mixture of butter, sugar, and eggs. Use room-temperature butter and a high setting on an electric mixer. Then, when you begin to add the flour, reduce the speed to low and mix the ingredients only until the flour disappears. If you mix any longer, the protein in the flour will become overworked and strengthened, causing the cake to be tough and not rise as high as you would like. Plus the texture will be uneven, with tunnels throughout.

- **ANGEL, CHIFFON, AND SPONGE CAKES:** A high cake that stands up even and straight is the winning feature here. First, the egg whites must be beaten with the sugar, until the sugar dissolves thoroughly. Stop beating as soon as the whites stand up in stiff, straight peaks. Most recipes include a small amount of cream of tartar, which helps to stabilize the egg whites. If you either underbeat or overbeat the whites, the cake will not rise to its maximum capacity and beauty. The texture should be even, without a compact "collapsed" layer at the bottom—this often results from the cake having "fallen" when you take it out of the oven too soon. Leave the cake in the oven until the top springs back when you touch it lightly.

## DECORATED TO LOOK LIKE A WINNER!

After the cake's frosted and decorated, it must be a showpiece! Here are a few secrets the best cooks know and use:

# Cooking Basics

## EASY ICE CREAM CAKES

With an ice cream cake in the freezer, an easy foolproof dessert's always at your fingertips. Even if you're not a baker, ice cream cakes are one of the easiest never-fail cakes you can make. Begin by making (or buying) a loaf pound cake (approximately 9 × 5 × 3 inches). Using a serrated knife, slice it horizontally into 5 layers. Then fill it with ice cream that has softened at room temperature for about 15 to 30 minutes, and frost all over with sweetened whipped cream. Cover it with a bubble of plastic wrap and freeze. When ready to serve, let stand at room temperature about 15 minutes before slicing. Here are a few great flavor variations:

**PEACH MELBA CAKE:** Fill alternating layers with peach ice cream and rich French vanilla ice cream (you'll need a pint of each). As you build the cake, sprinkle some raspberries over each ice cream layer before topping with the next layer of cake (you'll need 2 cups of fresh raspberries in all). Be sure to save some berries to top each serving. Then whip up a pint of heavy cream and flavor it with 2 tablespoons confectioners' sugar, 2 teaspoons vanilla extract, and ¼ teaspoon almond extract. Swirl it on the top and sides of the cake, then wrap and freeze. Before serving, top each slice with a few extra berries.

**MAPLE-NUT CAKE:** Spread vanilla ice cream between the layers (you'll need a quart). As you build the cake, drizzle each layer of cake with 1 tablespoon maple syrup and sprinkle with 2 tablespoons chopped walnuts. A pint of heavy cream whipped with 2 tablespoons confectioners' sugar, 2 teaspoons vanilla extract, and ½ teaspoon maple flavoring makes a great topping. Swirl it on the top and sides of the cake, and sprinkle the top with more chopped walnuts, then wrap and freeze.

**BLACK-OUT CAKE:** Start with a chocolate marble pound cake (or a regular buttery one if you can't find marble). Fill alternating layers with chocolate and chocolate swirl ice cream (you'll need about a pint of each). As you build the cake, sprinkle each layer of ice cream with 2 tablespoons chopped toasted pecans. A pint of heavy cream whipped with 2 tablespoons confectioners' superfine sugar and 1 tablespoon vanilla extract are a delicious topping to this delicious cake. Swirl it on the top and sides of the cake, sprinkle the top with more chopped toasted pecans, and dust with a little cocoa. Wrap and freeze.

- **LAYER CAKES:** Before frosting, level (even out) the layers to remove the "crown" (this is important not only for the bottom layer but also the top one if it's being decorated). Use a serrated knife and a sawing motion to make the cake layers completely flat on the top (go ahead, eat the extras!). Then, before applying that first swirl of frosting, brush away all the crumbs with a soft pastry brush and place the bottom layer on a serving plate. To keep the plate clean, cover the exposed edge with strips of waxed paper, tucking the paper beneath the cake to catch any drips. After frosting, just slip out the paper strips with any frosting drips on top, leaving the plate sparkling clean.

- **ANGEL FOOD, SPONGE, AND CHIFFONS:** Here again, brush away all those crumbs, especially on the side, before glazing or frosting. When glazing these cakes, use a small spoon to slowly drip the glaze down the side in decorative drizzles.
- **UPSIDE-DOWN CAKES:** In order for these to turn out picture perfect, carefully design the fruits and nuts on the bottom of the pan or skillet before spooning in the batter. Think color when choosing the fruits, and be sure to follow the recipe exactly for the glaze—too much sugar or not enough butter can result in the decorations sticking to the pan and not transferring to the cake.

## A PIECRUST THAT WINS FIRST PRIZE!

- **FOR THE MOST TENDER CRUST,** add a tablespoon of sugar to the dough. This prevents the proteins in the flour from forming strands of gluten, resulting in tough pastry. To further ensure tender pastry, cut the fat into the flour well with a pastry blender or two forks, until it's the size of small peas, and replace a tablespoon of water with either lemon juice (an acid) or sour cream (also an acid) to bind the dough together. And remember, the less you handle pie pastry, the more tender it will be.
- **FOR THE FLAKIEST CRUST,** use equal amounts of shortening and ¼- to ½-inch diced cold butter (larger pieces melt more slowly to create flakier layers). Also ice water will keep the fat firmer longer as the pastry bakes, further allowing flaky layers to form.
- **FOR A CRISP BOTTOM CRUST IDEAL FOR CREAM PIES,** bake it "blind" first (without a filling): To hold the crust's shape during baking, shape and flute the crust and chill it in the freezer for 15 minutes. Line the pastry with parchment or foil and fill it with pie weights, uncooked rice, or raw beans. Bake for 15 minutes in a preheated 400°F oven, then remove the parchment and weights and bake 5 minutes longer. Finally, brush with a little cream or egg yolk beaten with water and bake 5 more minutes to set the glaze. Now the crust is ready for its cream filling.

## A WINNING APPLE PIE!

Before adding the filling to the unbaked pie shell, sprinkle the bottom crust with a few bread crumbs; they absorb any extra liquid and keep the crust nice and crispy. You can bake an apple pie in a third less time (sometimes half) by slicing the apples about ¼-inch thick and sautéing them in a little butter in a skillet. Then toss them with the sugar and flavorings called for in your recipe

*Brownie Bottom Pudding Pie, page 53*

## Cooking Basics

### 4 FAST CRUMB CRUSTS

Anyone with a food processor can make a crumb crust in minutes. The best thing about these crusts is their use of graham crackers, vanilla wafers, or chopped nuts that are easy to keep on hand in the pantry. To make a crumb crust by hand, turn the wafers or crackers into crumbs by crushing them in a resealable plastic bag with a rolling pin.

Each of the recipes here makes enough for one shell—an 8- or 9-inch piecrust or a 10-inch tart shell.

**SNAPPY GINGER CRUST**
Place 40 gingersnaps, ¼ cup superfine sugar, and 1 teaspoon grated lemon zest in the food processor. Process to fine crumbs, then add ½ cup melted butter while the machine is running. Press into a buttered pie plate, then freeze for 15 minutes before baking in a 350°F oven for 8 to 10 minutes, or until set. This is the ideal crust for a banana cream pie.

**CINNAMONY GRAHAM CRUST** Pulse 10 large graham crackers (buy the cinnamony ones if you can find them), ¼ cup superfine sugar, and ½ teaspoon ground cinnamon in the food processor. Process to fine crumbs, then add ½ cup melted butter while the machine is running. Press into a buttered pie plate, then freeze for 15 minutes before baking in a 350°F oven for 8 to 10 minutes, or until set. Cool before filling. This crust is perfect for a strawberry tart.

**TOASTED COCONUT CRUMB** Toast 1½ cups sweetened flaked coconut in a 350°F oven for 10 minutes, or until golden, stirring occasionally. Toss the coconut into the food processor with 30 vanilla wafers. Process to fine crumbs, then add ½ cup melted butter while the machine is running. Press into a buttered pie plate, then freeze for 15 minutes before filling. No baking needed! Fill with vanilla ice cream and top it off with sliced fresh strawberries on top.

**NO-BAKE SOUTHERN PECAN CRUST** Pulse 30 vanilla wafers, 1 cup pecans, 3 tablespoons superfine sugar, and ¼ teaspoon ground cinnamon in the food processor. Process to fine crumbs, then add ½ cup melted butter while the machine is running. Press into a buttered pie plate, then freeze for 15 minutes before filling. No baking needed! Perfect for a peach tart.

and mound them into the pie shell for baking. Follow your recipe for the temperature of the oven, and bake until the apples are fork-tender, the filling is bubbly, and the top crust is golden brown. Since you've partially precooked the apples, you'll find this takes less time than the recipe calls for.

### WHIPPING CREAM THAT KEEPS ITS SWIRLS

Here are a few blue ribbon tips about whipping cream well worth remembering!

- When buying cream for whipping, plan on double the volume when whipped (that is, 1 cup heavy cream makes 2 cups whipped).
- Look for a carton of heavy cream or whipping cream labeled "pasteurized," found in gourmet markets. Avoid "ultra-pasteurized" heavy cream for whip-

ping; even though it lasts longer before souring (it has been briefly heated to kill microorganisms); it doesn't whip as well or taste as fresh as the pasteurized.

- Chill the bowl and beaters before whipping the cream. (They chill fast in the freezer in 15 minutes.) Use cream straight from the refrigerator. (Be sure it's very cold!)
- Stabilize whipped cream with a little gelatin. This lets you swirl it, pipe it, even tote it without losing its shape. Here's how to stabilize 1 cup of heavy (whipping) cream. Sprinkle a teaspoon of unflavored gelatin over 4 teaspoons cold water in a microwaveable cup. Let it stand until the gelatin has softened. Then heat it in the microwave on Medium, or over hot water just until dissolved (don't let it boil, or you'll lower the gelatin's thickening power). Then whip the cream until it reaches medium consistency, pour in this lukewarm gelatin all at once, and continue beating just until soft peaks form and the cream clings to the sides of the bowl. Use the whipping cream immediately, then refrigerate the cake or pie until ready to serve.

Take a few moments to browse through *Blue Ribbon Cakes & Pies* and plan which one to try. Here are some favorites, each guaranteed to bring you winning praise from family and friends!

**Buttery Pound Cake (page 22)**

**Easy Peach Crisp (page 37)**

**Classic Strawberry Shortcake (page 18)**

**Red Velvet Cake (page 42)**

**Gone to Heaven Chocolate Pie (page 51)**

**Sand Castle Cake (page 68)**

**Blue Ribbon Apple Pie (page 92)**

**Star Spangled Cocoa Bundt (page 110)**

**Triple Chocolate Cheesecake (page 50)**

*Chocolate Cherry Valentine, page 122*

*Pumpkin Faces, page 117*

*Triple Chocolate Cheesecake, page 50*

Cinnamon Raisin Cake, page 25

# Everyday Cakes & Pies

No time to make dessert during the week? Think again, as you thumb through this chapter! If it's berry season, stir up a shortcake. Or make a cobbler, a crisp, or an upside-down cake any time of year—they all mix up in minutes and always prompt requests for seconds, especially when topped with a scoop of ice cream or dollop of whipped cream. Or roll up an ice cream cake, bake a pecan pie, or whip up a simple pound cake on the weekend—then keep slicing servings all week long! They're guaranteed to come out of the oven blue ribbon perfect if you follow these tried-and-true recipes and use the baking tips. So sit back, take a bite, and enjoy the compliments.

# Classic Strawberry Shortcake

*Prep* **20 minutes**   *Bake* **10 minutes**

| | |
|---|---|
| 2 | large eggs, separated |
| 2 | cups all-purpose flour |
| ¼ | cup sugar + extra for sprinkling and sweetening |
| 4 | teaspoons baking powder |
| ¼ | teaspoon salt |
| Dash | ground nutmeg |
| ½ | cup cold butter or margarine, cut into pieces |
| ½ | cup milk |
| 2 | baskets (1 pint each) fresh strawberries, stemmed and sliced |
| 1 | cup heavy cream |
| Fresh mint leaves (optional) | |

*It must be summer if strawberry shortcake is being served! The key to the most tender biscuits is using very cold butter and not overworking the dough. This recipe is easy—you don't even need a biscuit cutter.*

**LET'S BEGIN** Preheat the oven to 450°F. Grease a large cookie sheet. In a small bowl, lightly beat the egg whites with a fork. Set aside.

**MAKE THE SHORTCAKES** Sift the flour, the ¼ cup sugar, baking powder, salt, and nutmeg into a large bowl. Cut in the butter with a pastry cutter until the mixture resembles coarse crumbs. In a small bowl, blend the milk and egg yolks together with a fork. Stir into the butter mixture to make a soft dough. Divide the dough into 6 portions and form into balls. Transfer the balls to the cookie sheet. Pat each into 3-inch circles, moistening your fingers with some of the beaten whites. Brush the cakes with the whites. Lightly sprinkle with sugar.

**INTO THE OVEN** Bake for 10 to 12 minutes, until golden. Transfer the cakes to wire racks and cool completely. Sweeten the strawberries with sugar to taste. Whip the cream and sweeten to taste. Halve the cakes horizontally with a serrated knife. Place the bottom halves on 6 dessert plates. Cover with the sliced strawberries and cake tops. Top each with a generous spoonful of whipped cream, a few sliced berries, and garnish with fresh mint leaves, if you wish.

**Makes 6 servings**

*Per serving: 568 calories, 9g protein, 60g carbohydrates, 33g fat, 18g saturated fat, 168mg cholesterol, 420mg sodium*

# Strawberry Angel Shortcakes

*Prep* **25 minutes**   *Bake* **20 minutes**

- 1 package (16 ounces) angel food cake mix
- 3 baskets (1 pint each) fresh strawberries
- 3 tablespoons sugar
- ½ cup heavy cream, whipped and sweetened to taste
- ¾ cup prepared hot fudge sauce, at room temperature
- 2 tablespoons Amaretto liqueur or ¼ teaspoon almond extract

*Here's all of the delectable flavor and satisfaction of strawberry shortcake minus a lot of the calories, thanks to angel food cake mix and a generous amount of ripe, juicy strawberries.*

**LET'S BEGIN** Preheat the oven to 350°F. Prepare the cake mix according to package directions. Spoon ½ cup batter into each of 8 ungreased 6-ounce ovenproof custard cups, filling each no more than two-thirds full. (Spoon the remaining batter into an ungreased 9 × 5-inch loaf pan and refrigerate.) Arrange the cups 2 inches apart on a large cookie sheet.

**INTO THE OVEN** Bake for 20 to 25 minutes, until the tops are dark golden brown. Cool the cups completely on wire racks. With a thin sharp knife, remove the cakes from the cups and halve horizontally with a serrated knife.

Meanwhile, bake the loaf cake for 35 minutes, or until the top is dark golden brown. Cool, remove from the pan according to package directions, and reserve for another use.

**ASSEMBLE** Reserve 8 of the strawberries with caps, for garnish. Stem and slice the remaining strawberries into a bowl. Sweeten with sugar to taste, cover, and refrigerate. Combine the fudge sauce and Amaretto in a small saucepan and stir over medium-low heat for about 3 minutes, just until warm. Spoon 1½ tablespoons of the fudge sauce onto each of 8 dessert plates. Place the bottom halves of the cakes on the plates. Cover with the sliced strawberries and cake tops. Spoon more sliced strawberries over the cakes. Top each with 2 tablespoons of the whipped cream and garnish with a whole strawberry.

*Makes 8 servings*

*Per serving: 349 calories, 6g protein, 61g carbohydrates, 10g fat, 5g saturated fat, 20mg cholesterol, 305mg sodium*

# Berry Sour Cream Shortcake

*Prep* **20 minutes**   *Bake* **20 minutes**

## SHORTCAKE

- 2 cups all-purpose flour
- ¼ cup sugar
- 2 teaspoons baking powder
- ½ teaspoon salt
- ¼ teaspoon baking soda
- ⅓ cup cold butter
- ½ cup sour cream
- 1 large egg
- ⅓ cup milk
- ½ teaspoon almond extract

## FRUIT

- 4 cups fresh fruit (sliced peaches and/or raspberries)
- ½ cup sugar
- 2 tablespoons Amaretto liqueur (optional)

Sweetened whipped cream (optional)

*No need to take out your biscuit cutters for this buttery shortcake. It is baked as one large shortcake in a round cake pan, then cut into wedges for serving. What a smart idea!*

**LET'S BEGIN** To make the shortcake, preheat the oven to 400°F. Grease a 9-inch round cake pan. Combine the flour, sugar, baking powder, salt, and baking soda in a large bowl. Cut in the butter with a pastry cutter until the mixture resembles coarse crumbs. Combine the sour cream and egg in a small bowl, then stir in the milk and almond extract and mix well. Add the sour cream mixture to the flour mixture and stir well. Spoon the batter into the pan.

**INTO THE OVEN** Bake for 20 to 25 minutes, until golden brown. Cool in the pan for 10 minutes. Remove the shortcake from the pan and cool completely on a wire rack.

**FILL & SERVE** To make the fruit, meanwhile, combine the fruit and sugar in a large bowl. Stir in the liqueur, if desired. Cover and refrigerate until serving time. To serve, cut the shortcake into 8 wedges. For each serving, use a serrated knife to split a wedge in half. Place the bottom half on a serving plate. Spoon ¼ cup of the fruit mixture over the cake and top with the remaining shortcake wedge. Spoon another ¼ cup of the fruit mixture on top. Serve with whipped cream, if you wish.

*Makes 8 servings*

*Per serving: 330 calories, 6g protein, 53g carbohydrates, 12g total fat, 6g saturated fat, 55mg cholesterol, 390mg sodium*

# Buttery Pound Cake

*Prep* **20 minutes**   *Bake* **55 minutes**

- 2 cups granulated sugar
- 1 cup butter, softened
- 5 large eggs
- ¼ cup sour cream
- ¼ cup milk
- 1 teaspoon vanilla extract
- 2¼ cups all-purpose flour
- ½ teaspoon salt
- Confectioners' sugar (optional)

This wonderful classic pound cake gets all of its height from sufficiently aerated butter and sugar and thoroughly beaten eggs.

**LET'S BEGIN** Preheat the oven to 350°F. Grease and flour a 12-cup Bundt cake pan or 10-inch tube pan.

**MIX IT UP** Beat the granulated sugar and the butter in a large bowl with an electric mixer on medium speed, scraping the bowl often, until light and fluffy. Add the eggs, one at a time, beating well after each addition. Beat in the sour cream, milk, and vanilla, scraping the bowl often, until well mixed. Reduce the speed to low and add the flour and salt just until blended. Spoon the batter into the pan.

**INTO THE OVEN** Bake for 55 to 65 minutes, until a wooden toothpick inserted in the center comes out clean. Cool in the pan for 15 minutes. Turn upside down onto a wire rack and remove the pan. Cool completely. Sprinkle with the confectioners' sugar, if you wish.

*Makes 12 servings*

*Per serving: 390 calories, 6g protein, 52g carbohydrates, 19g total fat, 9g saturated fat, 135mg cholesterol, 290mg sodium*

# CHERRY-MALLOW CAKE

Prep **15 MINUTES**    Bake **30 MINUTES**

- **4** cups miniature marshmallows
- **1** package (18.25 ounces) yellow cake mix
- **1** can (21 ounces) cherry pie filling and topping

*Just a cake mix and a can of cherry pie filling puts you on the path to an adult- and kid-pleasing dessert. Allowing the cake to cool completely gives the marshmallows time to set up for easy serving.*

**LET'S BEGIN** Preheat the oven to 350°F. Coat a 13 × 9-inch baking pan with nonstick cooking spray.

**ASSEMBLE** Spread the marshmallows evenly in the bottom of the pan. Prepare the cake mix batter according to package directions. Pour the batter over the marshmallows. Spoon the cherry pie filling evenly over the batter.

**INTO THE OVEN** Bake for 30 to 40 minutes, until the top of the cake is bubbly (the marshmallows will be sticky). Cool completely on a wire rack.

*Makes 15 servings*

*Per serving: 300 calories, 3g protein, 52g carbohydrates, 9g fat, 2g saturated fat, 44mg cholesterol, 258mg sodium*

# Fabulous Carrot Cake

*Prep* **15 minutes**   *Bake* **40 minutes**

- 3 cups all-purpose flour
- 2 teaspoons baking soda
- 1 teaspoon each ground cinnamon and ginger
- ½ teaspoon salt
- 1 cup margarine, softened
- 1 cup firmly packed brown sugar
- 1 cup granulated sugar
- 4 large eggs
- 1 can (20 ounces) crushed pineapple, well drained
- 4 cups shredded carrots
- 1 cup raisins
- 2 teaspoons vanilla extract
- Lemony Cream Cheese Frosting (see recipe)

*Almost everyone loves carrot cake. It can always be counted on to be moist, tender, and tasty. And lots of grated carrots make it healthy, too. Crushed pineapple makes these mini cakes extra moist and flavorful without extra work.*

**LET'S BEGIN** To make the cake, preheat the oven to 350°F. Grease and flour five 5 × 3-inch mini loaf pans. Combine the flour, baking soda, cinnamon, ginger, and salt in a medium bowl. Beat the margarine, brown sugar, and granulated sugar in a large bowl with an electric mixer on medium-high speed until light and fluffy. Beat in the eggs, one at a time, beating well after each addition. Beat in the pineapple, carrots, raisins, and vanilla. Reduce the speed to low, gradually add the flour mixture, and beat until well blended. Pour the batter into the pans.

**INTO THE OVEN** Bake for 40 minutes, or until a wooden toothpick inserted in the center comes out clean. Cool the cakes in the pans for 15 minutes. Unmold onto wire racks and cool completely.

## Lemony Cream Cheese Frosting

*To make the Frosting, beat 8 ounces of softened cream cheese and ½ cup of softened margarine in a large bowl with an electric mixer until smooth. Beat in 1½ cups of confectioners' sugar with 1 tablespoon lemon juice and 1 teaspoon grated lemon peel until light and fluffy. Spread the frosting over the cakes. Garnish with additional crushed pineapple and shredded carrots, if you wish.*

Makes 20 servings
Per serving: 387 calories, 5g protein, 57g carbohydrates, 17g fat, 4g saturated fat, 36mg cholesterol, 427mg sodium

# Cinnamon Raisin Cake

*Prep* **15 minutes**    *Bake* **55 minutes**

- 2 cups firmly packed light brown sugar
- 1½ cups all-purpose flour
- 1 cup whole wheat flour
- 2 teaspoons baking powder
- 2 teaspoons ground cinnamon
- 1½ teaspoons ground allspice
- 1 teaspoon ground nutmeg
- 1 teaspoon salt
- ½ teaspoon baking soda
- 1 cup milk
- ¾ cup vegetable oil
- ¼ cup orange juice
- 3 large eggs
- 2 teaspoons vanilla extract
- ¾ cup raisins
- ½ cup walnuts, chopped

### CARAMEL GLAZE

- ½ cup firmly packed light brown sugar
- ¼ cup butter
- 3 tablespoons light cream
- ⅛ teaspoon salt
- 1 cup confectioners' sugar
- ½ teaspoon vanilla extract
- Crystallized ginger, chopped (optional)

*The list of ingredients for this tube-pan cake is a bit long, but the flavor is spectacular and the prep is very short. You can prepare the dry ingredients in advance by combining them in a large resealable plastic bag.*

**LET'S BEGIN** Preheat the oven to 350°F. Grease a 10-inch tube pan. Combine the first 9 ingredients in a large bowl with an electric mixer on low speed. Add the milk, oil, orange juice, eggs, and vanilla and beat until the ingredients are moistened. Increase the speed to high and beat for 2 minutes. Fold in the raisins and walnuts. Pour into the pan.

**INTO THE OVEN** Bake for 55 minutes, until the sides of the cake are brown and pull away from the pan. Cool in the pan for 20 minutes. Turn upside down onto a wire rack and remove from the pan. Cool completely.

**GLAZE IT** To make the caramel glaze, combine the first 4 ingredients in a medium saucepan. Bring to a boil, stirring constantly. Cool slightly and whisk in the confectioners' sugar and vanilla. Spoon over the cake. Garnish with crystallized ginger, if you wish. Let the cake stand until the glaze is set.

*Makes 12 servings*
*Per serving: 563 calories, 6g protein, 84g carbohydrates, 24g fat, 5g saturated fat, 68mg cholesterol, 387mg sodium*

## On the Menu

Welcome spring with this easy make-ahead brunch menu that is sure to please friends and family alike.

Raspberry Orange Coolers

Asparagus & Red Pepper Frittata

Bacon Spirals

Drop Cheddar Biscuits

Long-Stemmed Strawberries

Chocolate Almond Coffee Cake

# APPLE CINNAMON CAKE

Prep **10 MINUTES**   Bake **30 MINUTES**

*Here's homemade cake for dessert that takes just 10 minutes to stir up from a cake mix and a can of pie filling. So easy!*

| 1 | tablespoon sugar |
| 1 | teaspoon ground cinnamon |
| 1 | package (18.25 ounces) spice or yellow cake mix |
| 1 | can (21 ounces) apple or peach fruit filling or topping |
| 3 | large eggs |

**LET'S BEGIN** Preheat the oven to 350°F. Grease a 13 × 9-inch baking pan. Combine the sugar and cinnamon in a cup.

**MIX IT UP** Combine the cake mix, fruit filling, and eggs in a large bowl. Beat with an electric mixer on medium speed for 2 minutes. Spread half the batter in the pan and sprinkle with half the cinnamon sugar. Repeat with the remaining batter and cinnamon sugar.

**INTO THE OVEN** Bake for 30 to 35 minutes, until a wooden toothpick inserted in the center comes out clean. Cool completely on a wire rack.

Makes 12 servings

Per serving: 260 calories, 4g protein, 48g carbohydrates, 6g fat, 1g saturated fat, 54mg cholesterol, 323mg sodium

# Ice Cream Cake Roll

*Prep* **30 minutes + freezing**   *Bake* **20 minutes**

- 1 package (16 ounces) angel food cake mix
- 1 pint coffee ice cream, softened
- 1 pint rum raisin ice cream, softened
- 1 package (12 ounces) semisweet chocolate chips
- ½ cup heavy cream

*Cake rolls are fun to make. For easiest serving, cut the cake roll with a long, thin knife that has been dipped briefly into hot water.*

**LET'S BEGIN** Preheat the oven to 350°F. Line the bottom of a 10 × 15-inch jelly-roll pan with parchment paper. Lightly coat the paper with nonstick cooking spray. Prepare the cake mix according to package directions. Spoon 4 cups of the batter into the pan and spread evenly.

**INTO THE OVEN** Bake for 20 minutes, until the top is golden brown. Cool in the pan for 15 minutes. Gently run a knife around the edge of the cake to loosen. Invert the cake onto a large wire rack. Remove the pan and gently peel off the parchment paper. Let cake cool completely on rack.

**FILL & ROLL** Line a large cookie sheet with parchment paper. Invert the cake crust side down onto the parchment. Spread the coffee ice cream over the top of the cake, leaving a ¼-inch border. Freeze for about 30 minutes, until the ice cream is firm. Spread the rum raisin ice cream over the coffee ice cream. Freeze for about 30 minutes, until the ice cream is firm. Working quickly, roll up the cake from one long side, pressing your fingers to start the roll. Transfer, seam side down, to a cookie sheet. Freeze for 2 hours, until firm.

**GLAZE** Melt the chocolate chips in a double boiler over simmering water. Add the cream and heat, stirring until smooth. Pour the glaze into a large glass measure. Transfer the roll to a wire rack set over a sheet of waxed paper. Pour the warm glaze over the roll to cover. Freeze the roll for 30 minutes, until the glaze is firm.

*Makes 10 servings*

*Per serving: 560 calories, 9g protein, 77g carbohydrates, 27g fat, 16g saturated fat, 100mg cholesterol, 430mg sodium*

28  BLUE RIBBON CAKES & PIES

# Pineapple Upside-Down Cake

Prep **30 minutes**   Bake **30 minutes**

Pineapple Upside-Down Cake is a true American creation. Most food historians believe that home cooks began baking them around 1926, about the same time that canned pineapple rings became available.

## TOPPING

- ¼ cup butter, melted
- ½ cup firmly packed brown sugar
- 2 cans (8 ounces each) sliced pineapple, packed in juice, well-drained
- 8 maraschino cherry halves (optional)

## CAKE

- 1½ cups all-purpose flour
- 2 teaspoons baking powder
- ¼ teaspoon salt
- ⅔ cup firmly packed brown sugar
- ⅓ cup butter, softened
- 2 large eggs
- 1½ teaspoons vanilla extract
- ½ cup milk

**LET'S BEGIN** Preheat the oven to 350°F. To make the topping, combine the butter and brown sugar in an 11 × 7-inch ungreased glass baking dish. Spread the mixture evenly in the dish. Arrange 8 pineapple slices on top. Place a cherry half in the center of each pineapple slice, if you wish.

**MIX IT UP** To make the cake, combine the flour, baking powder, and salt in a medium bowl. Beat the brown sugar and butter in a large bowl with an electric mixer on medium speed, scraping the bowl often, until creamy. Add the eggs, one at a time, beating well after each addition. Beat in the vanilla. Reduce the speed to low. Gradually add the flour mixture alternately with the milk, scraping the bowl often and beating well after each addition. Gently spread the batter over the pineapple.

**INTO THE OVEN** Bake for 30 to 40 minutes, until a wooden toothpick inserted in the center comes out clean. Immediately loosen the cake by running a knife around the inside edge of the dish. Invert the cake onto a serving platter and let stand 5 minutes. Remove the dish and cool completely.

*Makes 8 servings*
*Per serving: 390 calories, 5g protein, 60g carbohydrates, 16g total fat, 8g saturated fat, 90mg cholesterol, 370mg sodium*

## Peach Upside-Down Cake

*Substitute one 15-ounce can peach slices packed in juice (well drained) for the pineapple.*

## Cook to Cook

### HOW CAN I KEEP CAKE FRESH?

"It's easy to keep a delicious home-baked cake fresh, though different cakes need to be stored differently. Here's all you need to know to be able to enjoy baked treats day after day.

*Frosted Cakes and Cheesecakes* Be sure to refrigerate cakes that have fillings or frostings that contain dairy products, such as cream, eggs, sour cream, or yogurt.

*Butter Cakes* Due to their high fat content, these cakes remain fresh tasting for up to 3 days at room temperature.

*Foam Cakes (angel food, chiffon, and sponge cakes)* These contain little or no fat, so they dry out more quickly. Store them for up to 2 days at room temperature.

*Fruit Cakes* These contain dried fruits or brandy, so they can be kept at room temperature for at least a week when stored in a tightly closed container, such as a cake tin. Fresh fruit cakes will keep for up to 3 days."

## SuperQuick
# LIGHT SPICE CUPCAKES

*Prep* **5 MINUTES**    *Bake* **18 MINUTES**

*Did you know that mace and nutmeg are related? Mace is the bright red membrane that covers the nutmeg seed. Once it is removed from the seed, it is dried and ground. Its flavor is slightly more pungent than nutmeg.*

| | |
|---|---|
| 1 | package (18.25 ounces) yellow cake mix |
| 1¼ | cups water |
| ⅓ | cup vegetable oil |
| 3 | large eggs |
| 2 | teaspoons vanilla extract |
| 1 | teaspoon ground ginger |
| ¼ | teaspoon ground mace |
| 1 | tub (16 ounces) prepared frosting (optional) |

**LET'S BEGIN** Preheat the oven to 350°F. Grease or line twenty-four 2- to 3-inch muffin cups with paper liners and set aside.

**MIX IT UP** Beat the cake mix, water, oil, eggs, vanilla, ginger, and mace in a large bowl with an electric mixer on low speed for 30 seconds until moistened. Increase the speed to medium and beat for 2 minutes. Spoon the batter into muffin cups.

**INTO THE OVEN** Bake for 18 to 23 minutes, until a wooden toothpick inserted in the center comes out clean. Cool the cupcakes in the pans for 10 minutes. Unmold onto wire racks and cool completely. Spread the cupcakes with frosting, if you wish.

*Makes 2 dozen cupcakes*

Per cupcake: 121 calories, 1g protein, 18g carbohydrates, 5g fat, 1g saturated fat, 27mg cholesterol, 143mg sodium

# Banana Tarts

*Prep* **25 minutes**  *Bake* **15 minutes**

- 1 package (17¼ ounces) frozen puff pastry, thawed
- 4 large ripe bananas
- 1 cup turbinado sugar

*Store-bought puff pastry makes these tarts easy and special. It is available in supermarkets and specialty food stores. Be sure to thaw the puff pastry in the refrigerator as the package directs for the best results.*

**LET'S BEGIN** Preheat the oven to 375°F. Line 2 large cookie sheets with parchment paper.

**CUT OUT & ASSEMBLE** On a lightly floured surface, roll 1 sheet of puff pastry ⅛-inch thick. With a 4-inch-round cookie cutter, cut out 4 rounds of puff pastry. Transfer all 4 to one of the cookie sheets and prick well with a fork. Repeat rolling and cutting the remaining sheet of puff pastry into 4 more pastry rounds, transfer to the remaining cookie sheet, and prick with a fork. For each tart, thinly slice half a banana on an angle and arrange circles of overlapping banana slices on 1 puff pastry round, leaving a ¼-inch border. Repeat the process with the remaining bananas and puff pastry. Sprinkle each tart with 2 tablespoons sugar.

**INTO THE OVEN** Bake for 15 minutes, or until the pastry is golden brown. Transfer to wire racks to cool.

*Makes 8 tarts*
*Per tart: 482 calories, 5g protein, 65g carbohydrates, 23g fat, 6g saturated fat, 0mg cholesterol, 250mg sodium*

# Extreme Banana Cream Pie

*Prep* **20 MINUTES + THAWING**   *Bake* **18 MINUTES + CHILLING**

- 1 package (18 ounces) refrigerated chocolate morsels cookie bar dough, softened
- 1 bottle (16 ounces) banana-flavored refrigerated ready-to-drink milk
- 1 package (6-serving size) banana cream or vanilla instant pudding and pie filling mix
- 1 container (8 ounces) frozen whipped topping, thawed
- 2 ripe medium bananas, sliced

*Calling all banana lovers! Here's a pie with a triple dose of bananas. If you like, grate semisweet chocolate over the top.*

**LET'S BEGIN** Preheat the oven to 350°F. Grease a 9-inch pie pan. Break apart 15 squares of the cookie bar dough and press onto the bottom and up the sides of the pan. (You will have 5 squares left. Refrigerate for future use or bake and enjoy!) Bake for 18 to 24 minutes, until golden brown. Flatten down with the back of a spoon to form a piecrust. Cool completely on a wire rack.

**BEAT IT** Beat the milk, pudding mix, and half the whipped topping in a large bowl with an electric mixer on low speed until combined. Increase the speed to high and beat for 2 minutes until thick.

**ASSEMBLE** Arrange half the banana slices over the bottom of the crust. Pour half the pudding mixture over the bananas. Top with the remaining sliced bananas. Pour the remaining pudding mixture over the bananas. Spread the top with the remaining whipped topping. Refrigerate for 2 hours, or until firm.

Makes 8 servings

*Per serving: 430 calories, 4g protein, 66g carbohydrates, 16g fat, 8g saturated fat, 23mg cholesterol, 483mg sodium*

---

## Baking Basics

### CREAM PIE PERFECTION!

Here are some easy tips to ensure your next cream pie is perfection!

- Use a heavy saucepan or a double boiler to cook the custard cream.
- Stir the dry cornstarch (or flour) and sugar together before stirring in the milk.
- Stir the custard with a wooden spoon.
- Temper the egg yolks before adding them to the batter: Stir a little of the hot thickened milk mixture into the egg yolks, then slowly pour them back into the milk mixture, stirring fast to prevent scrambled eggs.
- To prevent a skin from forming on the custard as it cools, place plastic wrap directly on the surface of the pie. Refrigerate it until completely chilled.

# Classic Southern Pecan Pie

*Prep* **10 minutes**  *Bake* **45 minutes**

- 1 (9-inch) unbaked pie shell
- 4 large eggs
- 1 package (16 ounces) light brown sugar
- ¾ cup water
- 1 cup pecan halves
- ¼ cup butter or margarine, softened
- 1 teaspoon vanilla extract

*Pies become classics for good reason—they are pretty fabulous and loved by all. Here, a generous amount of pecans and a good dose of melted butter in the filling make this version especially delicious.*

**LET'S BEGIN** Preheat the oven to 350°F. Prepare the pie shell (do not bake).

**MAKE THE FILLING** Beat the eggs in a large bowl until frothy and set aside. Combine the sugar and water in a heavy 2-quart saucepan. Cook over medium heat, stirring, until the sugar dissolves. Bring to a full rolling boil and boil for 3 minutes. Gradually stir the hot syrup into the eggs. Stir in the pecans, butter, and vanilla until the butter melts. Pour the filling into the pie shell.

**INTO THE OVEN** Bake for 45 to 50 minutes, until the center of the filling is set. Cool completely on a wire rack.

*Makes 8 servings*

Per serving: 515 calories, 6g protein, 68g carbohydrates, 26g fat, 7g saturated fat, 122mg cholesterol, 218mg sodium

## Baking Basics

### MAKING THE MOVE

When rolling out pastry for a pie, start with a pastry cloth and sleeve for the rolling pin. Then rub them in flour to prevent the pastry from sticking. Roll the pastry out evenly and thin, but not too thin. Now for the fun part: making the move from the counter to the pie plate.

Here's a simple, never-fail way to transfer the pastry: Loosely wrap the dough around a rolling pin and hold it over the pie plate. Then gently and slowly, unwrap the dough directly onto the plate. Using your fingers, pat the pastry into the plate. Be careful not to stretch it, as this will cause it to shrink during baking.

**EVERYDAY CAKES & PIES**

## SuperQuick
# Quick & Easy Fruit Cobbler

*Prep* **5 minutes**   *Bake* **20 minutes**

- 1 can (21 ounces) peach or apple fruit filling or topping
- 1 cup biscuit baking mix
- ¼ cup sugar
- ¼ cup milk
- 2 tablespoons butter or margarine, melted

*Flavorful—and easy—canned fruit filling and biscuit baking mix make quick work of this dessert. The biscuit dough is dropped on top of the fruit filling so you don't even have to roll or cut out biscuits. What a great idea!*

**LET'S BEGIN** Preheat the oven to 400°F. Spoon the fruit filling into an 8- or 9-inch square baking pan.

**TOPPING** Combine all of the remaining ingredients in a medium bowl with a fork until blended. Drop by spoonfuls on top of the filling.

**INTO THE OVEN** Bake for 20 to 25 minutes, until golden brown. Transfer to a wire rack. Serve warm.

*Makes 6 servings*

*Per serving: 260 calories, 2g protein, 47g carbohydrates, 8g fat, 3g saturated fat, 12mg cholesterol, 335mg sodium*

### Cook to Cook

**WHAT ARE SOME OF YOUR FAVORITE FRUITS TO TOSS INTO COBBLERS?**

"I'm always trying new combinations of fruits and flavorings for my cobblers. It really depends upon the season and what looks good in the market on any given day.

I tossed *fresh raspberries into my peach cobbler* recently, along with a splash of Framboise (that's the French raspberry brandy) and some slivered almonds on top. I served it warm with a little heavy cream—and not a spoonful was left!

Using *triple the berries* is another delicious way to bake a cobbler. I like to mix blueberries, blackberries, and raspberries together in one dish, along with a little lemon zest. Then I spice up the biscuit topping with cinnamon before dropping it on top of the filling.

In the fall, I love to make fresh apple cobblers. *My favorite apples to use are those that are sweet-tart.* A few to try are Empire, Rome Beauty, Cortlands, and Jonagold (a cross between a Jonathan and a Golden Delicious).

I usually buy a couple of kinds and mix them. I always toss a few pecans into my apple cobbler and replace half of the granulated sugar called for in the recipe with brown sugar.

In the winter, my favorite cobbler is made from *fresh ripe pears plus some raspberries* when I can find them. If I can't find fresh berries, I often substitute frozen ones, which work well too. For a depth of flavor, I add a sprinkling of mace or nutmeg."

# Simply Good Cobbler

Prep **20 minutes**   Bake **35 minutes**

- 2 cans (15.25 ounces each) tropical fruit salad, undrained
- 1½ teaspoons cornstarch
- 1 teaspoon grated lemon peel
- 1 tablespoon + ⅓ cup firmly packed brown sugar
- ½ cup chopped dates
- ½ cup all-purpose flour
- ½ cup quick-cooking oats
- 1 teaspoon ground cinnamon
- ¼ teaspoon ground ginger
- ¼ teaspoon ground nutmeg
- ¼ cup margarine, softened

*Oat-topped cobblers are special. The oats add just enough "chew" to be appealing, and it's good for you, too. This cobbler is cleverly made with easy canned tropical fruit salad—what a fabulous twist!*

**LET'S BEGIN** Preheat the oven to 350°F. Pour the fruit salad into a medium bowl and stir in the cornstarch, lemon peel, and the 1 tablespoon brown sugar until the cornstarch is dissolved. Pour into an 8-inch square baking dish. Sprinkle with the dates.

**TOP IT** Combine the flour, oats, cinnamon, ginger, nutmeg, and the remaining ⅓ cup brown sugar in a medium bowl. With a fork, blend in the margarine until crumbly, then sprinkle the dates over the cobbler.

**INTO THE OVEN** Bake for 35 minutes, or until hot and bubbly. Transfer to a wire rack and cool slightly before serving.

*Makes 9 servings*

*Per serving: 236 calories, 2g protein, 47g carbohydrates, 6g fat, 1g saturated fat, 0mg cholesterol, 65mg sodium*

# Apple Colby Crisp

Prep **20 minutes**   Bake **50 minutes**

| | |
|---|---|
| 2 | pounds tart apples (about 4 large), such as Granny Smith, Winesap, Northern Spy, or Jonathan, peeled, cored, and sliced |
| 1 | cup granulated sugar |
| 2 | teaspoons lemon juice |
| ½ | cup firmly packed light brown sugar |
| ½ | cup quick-cooking or old-fashioned oats |
| ¼ | cup all-purpose flour |
| ½ | teaspoon ground cinnamon |
| ½ | cup cold butter, cut into pieces |
| ¾ | cup shredded Colby cheese |

*Apples and cheese are a classic combo for a good reason—they're fabulous together! Use tart apples that hold their shape during baking and complement them with brown and granulated sugars.*

**LET'S BEGIN** Preheat the oven to 350°F. Combine the apples, ½ cup of the granulated sugar, and the lemon juice in a large bowl. Spread evenly in an 8-inch square baking dish.

**MIX IT UP** Combine the brown sugar, oats, flour, cinnamon, and the remaining ½ cup granulated sugar in a medium bowl. Cut in the butter with a pastry cutter until the mixture is crumbly. Stir in the cheese. Sprinkle the cheese mixture evenly over the apples.

**INTO THE OVEN** Bake for 50 to 60 minutes, until the apples are tender and the topping is browned. Transfer to a wire rack. Serve warm or at room temperature.

*Makes 6 servings*

Per serving: 550 calories, 7g protein, 84g carbohydrates, 23g fat, 12g saturated fat, 58mg cholesterol, 223mg sodium

## SuperQuick
# Easy Peach Crisp

*Prep* **5 minutes**  *Bake* **15 minutes**

- 2 cans (15¼ ounces each) sliced peaches, drained
- 2 packages (1.6 ounces each) cinnamon and spice instant oatmeal, uncooked
- ⅓ cup all-purpose flour
- ½ cup chopped walnuts
- ⅓ cup butter, melted
- Vanilla ice cream (optional)

*A crisp is comfort food at its best. It is easy to put together, it smells ever so enticing while baking, and it makes you feel good when you eat it. This crisp is great with walnuts, but if you happen to have hazelnuts or pecans in your pantry, they will be just as tasty.*

**LET'S BEGIN** Preheat the oven to 425°F. Lightly butter a 2-quart baking dish.

**FILL & SPRINKLE** Pour the peaches into the baking dish. Combine the uncooked oatmeal, flour, and walnuts in a bowl. Stir in the butter until the ingredients are evenly moistened. Sprinkle the oatmeal mixture evenly over the peaches.

**INTO THE OVEN** Bake for 15 minutes, or until golden brown. Cool on a wire rack. Serve warm with a scoop of vanilla ice cream, if you wish.

*Makes 6 servings*

*Per serving: 310 calories, 4g protein, 36g carbohydrates, 18g fat, 6g saturated fat, 28mg cholesterol, 169mg sodium*

---

## Time Savers

### 5 OTHER FAST FRUIT CRISPS

For a change of pace and taste, try a variation of the Apple Colby Crisp. Almost any fruit can be substituted for the apples, with a few minor adjustments to the flavorings. Use a total of 2 pounds of fresh fruit.

**PEARS:** Start with the ripest, juiciest pears you can find. Add a little grated fresh ginger and substitute ground ginger for the cinnamon in the topping.

**PLUMS:** If you haven't yet baked a plum tart, you're in for a big treat! Omit the lemon juice and toss in 1 or 2 tablespoons of orange marmalade with the plum slices. Substitute chopped almonds for the cheese.

**NECTARINES:** Add a cup of fresh or frozen thawed cranberries to nectarines. Add ⅛ teaspoon nutmeg to the cinnamon, and substitute pecan halves and dried cranberries for the cheese.

**BERRIES:** Use any combination of blueberries, raspberries, and blackberries. Substitute chopped walnuts for the cheese.

**CHERRIES:** Use pitted fresh or frozen cherries. If using frozen cherries, thaw and drain them. Omit the lemon juice. Substitute coarsely crushed vanilla wafers for the cheese.

# Almond Crunch Snack Cake

*Prep* **15 minutes**   *Bake* **25 minutes**

- 2 cups all-purpose flour
- 1 tablespoon baking powder
- ½ teaspoon salt
- ½ cup granulated sugar
- ½ cup vegetable oil
- 1 large egg
- ½ cup milk
- ½ cup chopped dates
- ½ cup orange juice
- 1 tablespoon grated orange peel
- **Crunch Topping (see recipe)**

*Sugar and spice and everything nice—that's what this snackin' cake is made of. Delicious!*

**LET'S BEGIN** Preheat the oven to 375°F. Grease a 9-inch square baking pan. Combine the flour, baking powder, and salt in a small bowl. Beat the granulated sugar, oil, egg, and milk in a large bowl with an electric mixer on medium speed until blended. Reduce the speed to low and stir in the flour mixture just until blended. Stir in the dates, orange juice, and orange peel just until blended. Spread the batter evenly in the pan.

**MAKE THE TOPPING** Combine all the ingredients for the topping in a medium bowl until crumbly, then sprinkle over the batter.

**INTO THE OVEN** Bake for 25 to 30 minutes, until a wooden toothpick inserted in the center of the cake comes out clean. Cool completely on a wire rack.

## Crunch Topping

*To make the Crunch Topping, combine ½ cup chopped natural, unblanched almonds with ½ cup firmly packed light brown sugar, 2 tablespoons softened butter or margarine, and 1 teaspoon ground cinnamon.*

**Makes 9 servings**

*Per serving: 415 calories, 6g protein, 55g carbohydrates, 20g fat, 3g saturated fat, 32mg cholesterol, 248mg sodium*

# Chocolate Almond Coffee Cake

Prep **25 minutes**   Cook **30 minutes**

Streusel Topping (see recipe)

| | |
|---|---|
| 2 | cups all-purpose flour |
| 1 | teaspoon baking powder |
| 1 | teaspoon baking soda |
| ½ | teaspoon salt |
| ¾ | cup butter or margarine, softened |
| ¾ | cup firmly packed brown sugar |
| ¼ | cup honey |
| 1 | teaspoon almond extract |
| 3 | large eggs |
| ½ | cup milk |
| 1½ | cups semisweet chocolate morsels |

Chocolate Glaze (see recipe)

Use a pastry blender to cut in the butter for the streusel topping.

**LET'S BEGIN** Preheat the oven to 350°F. Grease and flour two 9-inch round cake pans. Make the Streusel Topping.

**MIX IT UP** To make the cake, combine the flour, baking powder, baking soda, and salt in a small bowl. Beat the butter, brown sugar, honey, and almond extract in a large bowl with an electric mixer on medium-high speed until creamy. Add the eggs, one at a time, beating well after each addition. Reduce the speed to low, beat in the flour mixture alternately with the milk, beginning and ending with the flour mixture. Stir in the chocolate morsels. Divide the batter into the pans. Sprinkle with the streusel topping.

**BAKE & GLAZE** Bake for 20 to 30 minutes, until a wooden toothpick inserted in the center comes out clean. Cool in pans on wire racks for 15 minutes. Drizzle the glaze over the warm cakes. Cool completely.

## Streusel Topping

To make the Streusel Topping, combine ½ cup firmly packed brown sugar with ½ cup all-purpose flour in a medium bowl. Cut in ¼ cup butter or margarine with a pastry cutter until the mixture resembles coarse crumbs. Stir in ¾ cup sliced almonds and ½ cup semisweet chocolate morsels.

## Chocolate Glaze

To make the Chocolate Glaze, melt ½ cup semisweet chocolate morsels with 1 tablespoon butter or margarine and 1 tablespoon milk in a small, heavy saucepan over low heat, stirring until smooth.

*Makes 16 servings*

Per serving: 452 calories, 6g protein, 55g carbohydrates, 26g fat, 12g saturated fat, 75mg cholesterol, 285mg sodium

Choco-holic Cake, page 43

# Lots of Chocolate

Among the most prized blue ribbons in many competitions are those awarded for a chocolate pie or a fudge layer cake. The reason is simple: Everyone loves chocolate! Many cooks master baking their own heavenly chocolate cream pie or luscious chocolate cake, then proudly take it to the fair. Now's your chance to bake some fabulous ribbon-worthy desserts. Try the forever winning 3-Layer German Sweet Chocolate Cake, the Brownie Bottom Pudding Pie, or Mile High Chocolate Cake (it's baked in an angel food pan). Then get ready for the best reward—winning smiles from your family and friends.

# RED VELVET CAKE

*Prep* **30 MINUTES**     *Bake* **40 MINUTES + COOLING**

- 2¼ cups all-purpose flour
- 3 tablespoons unsweetened cocoa
- 1 teaspoon salt
- ¾ cup vegetable shortening
- 1⅔ cups sugar
- 2 large eggs
- 1 cup buttermilk
- 2 bottles (1 ounce each) red food coloring
- 1 teaspoon vanilla extract
- 1 teaspoon baking soda
- 1 teaspoon white vinegar
- Fluffy Buttercream Frosting (see recipe)

*This cake is as soft as red velvet.*

**LET'S BEGIN** Preheat the oven to 350°F. Grease and flour two 8- or 9-inch round cake pans or one 13 × 9-inch baking pan. To make the cake, combine the flour, cocoa, and salt in a large bowl. Beat the shortening, sugar, and eggs in a large bowl with an electric mixer on medium-high speed until light and fluffy. Beat in the buttermilk, food coloring, and vanilla until blended. Reduce the speed to low and beat in the flour mixture just until blended. Dissolve the baking soda in the vinegar in a small bowl and beat into the batter. Pour the batter into the pan(s).

**INTO THE OVEN** Bake for 35 to 40 minutes, until a wooden toothpick inserted in the center comes out clean. Cool the cakes in the pans for 10 minutes. Unmold onto wire racks and cool completely. Meanwhile, make the Buttercream Frosting and use it to frost the cake.

## FLUFFY BUTTERCREAM FROSTING

*Stir 1 cup milk and 2 tablespoons all-purpose flour constantly in a small saucepan over medium heat for 5 minutes, or until thickened. Remove from the heat. Cover with plastic wrap placed directly on the milk mixture (to prevent a skin from forming) and cool completely. Beat 1 cup softened butter (no substitutions, please!) and 1 cup sugar in a medium bowl with an electric mixer on medium-high speed until creamy. Beat 1 teaspoon vanilla extract and ½ teaspoon red food coloring, if you like. Beat in the cooled milk mixture until light, fluffy, and spreadable. If the frosting is too thin, refrigerate for 5 to 10 minutes and beat again. Fill and frost cake.*

**Makes 12 servings**
Per serving: 442 calories, 5g protein, 84g carbohydrates, 10g total fat, 5g saturated fat, 58mg cholesterol, 392mg sodium

# Choco-Holic Cake

Prep **15 MINUTES**   Bake **55 MINUTES + COOLING**

- 1 package (18.25 ounces) chocolate cake mix
- 1 package (3.4 ounces) chocolate instant pudding and pie filling mix
- 1 cup milk
- ½ cup sour cream
- 4 large eggs
- 1 package (12 ounces) semisweet chocolate morsels
- 1 cup chopped walnuts
- Confectioners' sugar (optional)
- Fresh raspberries (optional)

*Walnuts taste great in this really chocolatey cake, but you can also use pecans or almonds, if you happen to have them in your pantry.*

**LET'S BEGIN** Preheat the oven to 350°F. Grease and flour a 12-cup Bundt pan or 10-inch tube pan.

**MIX IT UP** Beat the first 5 ingredients in a large bowl with an electric mixer on low speed just until blended. Increase the speed to high and beat for 2 minutes. Stir in the chocolate morsels and walnuts. Pour into the cake pan.

**INTO THE OVEN** Bake for 55 to 65 minutes, until a wooden toothpick inserted in the center comes out clean. Cool in the pan for 20 minutes. Turn upside down onto a wire rack and remove the pan. Cool completely. Dust with the confectioners' sugar and garnish with raspberries, if you wish.

*Makes 16 servings*

*Per serving: 352 calories, 6g protein, 44g carbohydrates, 19g fat, 7g saturated fat, 57mg cholesterol, 383mg sodium*

---

## Cook to Cook

### WHAT MAKES RED VELVET CAKE TURN RED?

"It may surprise you to learn that this old-fashioned layer cake has been popular, especially in the South, since the 1940s. *It gets its vibrant color from the addition of red food coloring.* The amount of cocoa in recipes for this cake varies from a couple of tablespoons to ¼ cup, and the red coloring can be as little as 2 teaspoons or as much as a 2-ounce bottle, depending on how red you want your cake to be.

*Mix the cocoa with the red food coloring until the mixture is smooth.* This trick gives the cake the very best, uniform red color throughout. The authentic Red Velvet Cake has *a little white vinegar added to the batter.* Use apple cider vinegar or one of the fruit-flavored ones instead of the pungent white one.

Classically the layers are sandwiched with plenty of fluffy white frosting. The original frosting was a cooked white buttercream, but often a *7-minute white boiled frosting or a cream cheese frosting* is used instead. However you frost it, it's worthy of the name it's often called: *the hundred-dollar cake!*"

# Chocolate Angel Food Cake

*Prep* **10 minutes**   *Bake* **40 minutes + cooling**

- 1 package (14.5 to 16 ounces) angel food cake mix
- ½ cup unsweetened cocoa
- 2 tablespoons confectioners' sugar
- 1 cup fresh strawberries (optional)

*Chocolate angel food cake is just as light in texture—and calories—as plain angel food cake, but with the rich flavor of chocolate, thanks to unsweetened cocoa.*

**LET'S BEGIN** Preheat the oven according to the cake mix package directions.

**MIX IT UP** Prepare the cake mix batter according to the package directions, except add the cocoa to the dry ingredients.

**BAKE & SERVE** Bake the cake according to the directions. Sprinkle the cooled cake with the confectioners' sugar and serve with the strawberries, if you wish.

*Makes 12 servings*

*Per serving: 140 calories, 4g protein, 32g carbohydrates, 1g fat, 0g saturated fat, 0mg cholesterol, 253mg sodium*

---

## Baking Basics

### FIX-IT TIPS FOR ANGEL FOOD CAKES

Your angel food cake collapsed! It can't be salvaged. But it can be served. Tear it up into pieces and layer it with homemade custard and fresh sliced strawberries in a large glass dish. After you have accepted the compliments for a delicious dessert, read these fix-it tips to find out how to make sure your angel food cakes come out a winner from now on.

**If the egg whites wouldn't beat to a peak . . .**

- First make sure the bowl and the beaters are sparkling clean. If there's even a little bit of fat on either, this can prevent the egg whites from beating to peaks.
- As you separate the eggs, watch carefully that not even the smallest speck of egg yolk slips into the bowl of whites. The tiniest amount of yolk can cause the egg whites to only foam and never form stiff white peaks, regardless of how long you beat them.

**If the cake falls out of the pan while cooling . . .**

- Test the cake before removing it from the oven. It's done when the cake springs back when lightly touched or a wooden toothpick inserted comes out clean.
- Immediately turn the cake upside down to cool. Many tube pans have three little "legs" on the top rim for this purpose. If yours doesn't, invert the pan and slip the center tube over the top of a narrow-necked bottle so the cake is elevated.

# MIDNIGHT BLISS CAKE

*Prep* **10 MINUTES**    *Bake* **50 MINUTES + COOLING**

This decadent chocolate cake gets its moistness from the sour cream and vegetable oil.

- 1 package (18.25 ounces) chocolate cake mix
- 1 package (3-ounce size) chocolate instant pudding and pie filling mix
- ½ cup international coffee mix, any flavor
- 4 large eggs
- 1 container (8 ounces) sour cream
- ½ cup vegetable oil
- ½ cup water
- 1 package (8 ounces) semisweet baking chocolate (8 squares), chopped

Confectioners' sugar (optional)

**LET'S BEGIN** Preheat the oven to 350°F. Lightly grease a 12-cup Bundt cake pan or 10-inch tube pan.

**MIX IT UP** Beat the cake mix, pudding mix, coffee mix, eggs, sour cream, oil, and water in a large bowl with an electric mixer on low speed just until moistened, scraping the sides of the bowl frequently. Increase the speed to medium and beat for 2 minutes, or until well blended. Stir in the chopped chocolate. Spoon the batter into the pan.

**INTO THE OVEN** Bake for 50 to 60 minutes, until a wooden toothpick inserted near the center comes out clean. Cool in the pan for 10 minutes. Loosen the cake from the sides of the pan with a metal spatula or knife. Turn upside down onto a wire rack and remove the pan. Cool completely. Sprinkle with the confectioners' sugar, if you wish.

*Makes 18 servings*

Per serving: 330 calories, 4g protein, 39g carbohydrates, 19g fat, 6g saturated fat, 55mg cholesterol, 390mg sodium

---

### Cook to Cook

**HOW CAN I TELL WHEN THE CAKE IS DONE?**

"Telling when a cake is done depends somewhat on the type of cake you are baking. There are two kinds of cakes: foam cakes and butter cakes.

Foam cakes, such as *angel food and chiffon,* depend on beaten egg whites, egg yolks, or whole eggs for their light, airy textures. These cakes test done *when the top is golden and the cake springs back* when gently pressed with your finger.

Butter cakes rely on butter for their moist texture and rich flavor. These cakes test done when the top is lightly browned, *the edges begin to pull away from the sides of the pan,* and the top springs back when the center is gently pressed with your finger.

You can also insert a cake tester or wooden toothpick into the center of a butter cake. It should come out clean and dry when the cake is done, though some butter cakes, such as moist chocolate ones, are done when a few crumbs cling to the tester."

# MILE-HIGH CHOCOLATE CAKE

*Prep* **25 MINUTES**    *Bake* **45 MINUTES**

- 1 package (12 ounces) semisweet chocolate chips
- 7 large egg yolks
- ½ cup + 1 tablespoon honey
- 1⅔ cups (8 ounces) slivered almonds, toasted and ground + extra for sprinkling (optional)
- 12 large egg whites
- Pinch salt
- ¼ cup butter or margarine

*Be sure to beat the egg yolks and honey until really thick and lemon-colored. Depending on the type of mixer you are using, this may take a few minutes longer than the time indicated in the recipe. Don't worry. The important thing is not the amount of time it takes, but that they look right.*

**LET'S BEGIN** Preheat the oven to 350°F. In a food processor, finely ground 1⅓ cups of the chocolate chips. Set aside. Beat the egg yolks and ½ cup of the honey in a large bowl with an electric mixer until thick and lemon-colored, about 3 minutes. Stir in the ground chocolate and the almonds and set aside. Beat the egg whites in another large bowl with an electric mixer until foamy. Add the salt and continue to beat until stiff peaks form. With a rubber spatula, gently fold one-quarter of the whites into the chocolate mixture. Gently fold in the remaining whites just until blended. (Do not overmix.) Pour the batter into an ungreased 10-inch tube pan.

**INTO THE OVEN** Bake for 45 to 50 minutes, until a wooden toothpick inserted near the center comes out clean. Immediately invert the pan onto a funnel or bottle. Cool completely.

**GLAZE IT** Combine the butter, the remaining chocolate chips, and the remaining 1 tablespoon honey in the top of a double boiler set over simmering water. Stir until the mixture is melted and smooth. Let cool to thicken slightly. When the cake is cool, run a metal spatula or knife around the sides of the pan and tube. Invert the cake onto a serving plate and remove the pan. Pour or spread the glaze over the top, allowing the excess to drip down the sides. Let the cake stand until the glaze is set.

*Makes 12 servings*
*Per serving: 377 calories, 10g protein, 35g carbohydrates, 25g fat, 9g saturated fat, 130mg cholesterol, 112mg sodium*

# Chocolate Volcano

*Prep* **20 minutes**     *Bake* **20 minutes + chilling**

- 1 package (21.5 ounces) brownie mix
- 2½ cups fresh or frozen cranberries
- 1 cup sugar
- ¾ cup + 2 tablespoons water
- 2 tablespoons cornstarch
- 2 tablespoons salted peanuts, coarsely chopped
- ⅓ cup hot fudge topping, slightly warm

*Cranberries are great to have on hand. Stock up during the fall and winter when they are in season by popping several bags (just as they are) into your freezer. No need to thaw them before adding into baked goods such as cookies, muffins, or cakes. How easy is that?*

**LET'S BEGIN** Preheat the oven according to the brownie package directions. Grease a 9¼-inch quiche pan and an 8-inch square baking pan. Prepare the brownies as directed on the package except evenly spread half the batter in the quiche pan and the other half in the square pan. Bake for 20 minutes, or until a wooden toothpick inserted in the center comes out clean. Transfer to a wire rack and cool completely.

**MAKE FILLING** Meanwhile, combine the cranberries, sugar, and ¾ cup of the water in a medium saucepan. Bring to a boil, stirring occasionally. Reduce the heat and gently boil, stirring occasionally, for 10 minutes. Meanwhile, combine the cornstarch and the remaining 2 tablespoons water in a small bowl. Whisk into the cranberry mixture and boil 1 minute until thickened. Transfer the filling to a bowl. Refrigerate until thoroughly chilled.

**ASSEMBLE** Cut half the brownie in the square pan into ½-inch cubes. (Cut the other half into regular-sized brownies to enjoy later.) Spoon the cranberry filling over the brownie in the quiche pan. Sprinkle brownie cubes and peanuts on top. Drizzle with warmed hot fudge topping. Cut into wedges to serve.

**Makes 10 servings**

Per serving: 478 calories, 5g protein, 78g carbohydrates, 16g fat, 4g saturated fat, 41mg cholesterol, 283mg sodium

# 3-Layer German Sweet Chocolate Cake

*Prep* **30 minutes**   *Bake* **35 minutes + cooling**

## CAKE

- 1 package (4 ounces) German sweet chocolate
- ⅓ cup boiling water
- 2 cups sifted cake flour (not self-rising)
- ¾ teaspoon baking soda
- ¼ teaspoon salt
- ¾ cup butter or margarine, softened
- 1⅓ cups sugar
- 3 large eggs, separated
- ¾ teaspoon vanilla extract
- ¾ cup buttermilk

## COCONUT-PECAN FILLING & FROSTING

- 1 can (12 ounces) evaporated milk
- 1½ cups sugar
- ¾ cup butter or margarine
- 4 large egg yolks, lightly beaten
- 1½ teaspoons vanilla extract
- 1 package (7 ounces) sweetened flaked coconut
- 1½ cups chopped pecans

*German sweet chocolate was named after Samuel German, who created it for the Baker Chocolate Company in 1852.*

**LET'S BEGIN** Preheat the oven to 350°F. Line the bottoms of three 9-inch round cake pans with waxed paper. Combine the chocolate and boiling water in a medium bowl and stir until the chocolate is completely melted. Cool.

**MIX IT UP** Combine the flour, baking soda, and salt in a medium bowl. Beat the butter and sugar in a large bowl with an electric mixer on medium speed until light and fluffy. Add the egg yolks, one at a time, beating well after each addition. Stir in the melted chocolate and vanilla. Add the flour mixture alternately with the buttermilk, beginning and ending with the flour mixture and beating well after each addition. Beat the egg whites in a small bowl with an electric mixer with clean beaters on high speed until stiff peaks form. With a rubber spatula, gently fold into the batter. Pour evenly into the pans.

**BAKE & FROST** Bake for 35 minutes, or until a wooden toothpick inserted in the center comes out clean. Immediately loosen the cakes by running a knife around the inside edge of the pans. Cool in the pans for 15 minutes. Invert the cakes onto wire racks. Remove the pans and waxed paper. Cool completely. Meanwhile, to make the coconut-pecan filling & frosting, combine the evaporated milk, sugar, butter, egg yolks, and vanilla in a large saucepan. Cook, stirring constantly, over medium heat for 12 minutes, or until thickened and golden brown. Remove from the heat, add the coconut and pecans, and mix well. Cool to room temperature and to a desired spreading consistency. Spread the frosting between the layers and over the top of the cake.

*Makes 16 servings*

*Per serving: 565 calories, 7g protein, 58g carbohydrates, 35g fat, 17g saturated fat, 146mg cholesterol, 312mg sodium*

# Triple Chocolate Cheesecake

*Prep* **30 minutes**     *Bake* **1 hour + chilling**

## CRUST

- 1¼ cups chocolate wafer cookie crumbs (about 25 cookies)
- 3 tablespoons butter or margarine, melted

## FILLING

- 1¼ cups sugar
- ¼ cup unsweetened cocoa
- 2 containers (15 ounces each) light ricotta cheese
- ½ cup half-and-half
- ¼ cup all-purpose flour
- 1 teaspoon vanilla extract
- ¼ teaspoon salt
- 3 large eggs
- 1 ounce (1 square) white chocolate, melted according to package directions

*A chocolate wafer cookie crust, cocoa-flavored ricotta filling, and white chocolate drizzles make this recipe a keeper. White chocolate (which isn't technically chocolate) easily burns. So be sure to melt it as the package directs, or over very low heat.*

**LET'S BEGIN** Preheat the oven to 350°F. To make the crust, combine the cookie crumbs and butter in a small bowl until the crumbs are equally moistened. Press evenly over the bottom of an 8- or 9-inch springform pan. Bake for 10 minutes. Cool completely on a wire rack. (Leave the oven on.)

**MIX IT UP** Meanwhile, for the filling, combine the sugar and cocoa in a medium bowl and set aside. Beat the ricotta, half-and-half, flour, vanilla, and salt in a large bowl with an electric mixer on medium-high speed until smooth. Gradually add the sugar mixture and beat until smooth. Add the eggs, one at a time, beating well after each addition. Pour into the crust.

**BAKE & DECORATE** Bake for 1 hour, or until the center is set. Cool completely on a wire rack. Cover and refrigerate at least 4 hours or overnight. Just before serving, run a sharp knife around the edge to loosen the cake and remove the springform side of the pan. Place the white chocolate in a small resealable plastic bag and cut off one small corner of the bag. Drizzle the chocolate over the cake in a decorative pattern.

*Makes 8 servings*

*Per serving: 431 calories, 14g protein, 58g carbohydrates, 17g fat, 6g saturated fat, 113mg cholesterol, 364mg sodium*

# GONE TO HEAVEN CHOCOLATE PIE

*Prep* **10 MINUTES**   *Cook* **15 MINUTES + CHILLING**

*Be sure to chill this delicious pie for several hours to guarantee that the filling has had time to set up and thicken.*

| | |
|---|---|
| ⅔ | cup sugar |
| ⅓ | cup cornstarch |
| ½ | teaspoon salt |
| 4 | large egg yolks |
| 3 | cups milk |
| 2 | tablespoons butter or margarine, softened |
| 1 | tablespoon vanilla extract |
| 1 | package (12 ounces) dark chocolate chips |
| 1 | (9-inch) fully baked pie shell |

Sweetened whipped cream or whipped topping (optional)

**LET'S BEGIN** Combine the sugar, cornstarch, and salt in a 2-quart saucepan. Whisk the egg yolks and milk in a 1-quart glass measure or medium bowl. Gradually whisk the milk mixture into the sugar mixture until blended.

**COOK IT** Set the saucepan over medium heat and cook, stirring constantly, until the mixture comes to a boil. Boil and stir 1 minute. Remove the pan from the heat and stir in the butter and vanilla. Stir in 1¾ cups of the chocolate chips until the chips are melted and the mixture is well blended.

**CHILL & SERVE** Pour the filling into the pie shell and spread evenly. Press a sheet of plastic wrap directly on the surface of the filling. Cool to room temperature. Refrigerate the pie for several hours, until chilled and firm. Garnish with whipped cream, if you wish, and the remaining chips.

Makes 6 servings
Per serving: 690 calories, 10g protein, 84g carbohydrates, 38g fat, 18g saturated fat, 160mg cholesterol, 450mg sodium

## Cook to Cook

**HAS YOUR CHOCOLATE PIE EVER TURNED INTO CHOCOLATE SOUP?**

❝ There's nothing worse than making a lovely chocolate pie with a filling that's thick and rich, then cutting into it only to find the filling has turned into "soup"! *It liquefied as the pie cooled*—a chocolate disaster that has befallen many a cook.

Here's what happened: *Raw egg yolks contain an enzyme that loves to eat up starch.* And the custard filling of a cream pie is thickened with cornstarch, which is exactly the type of starch the enzyme loves. While your pie is chilling and setting overnight, the enzyme is quietly destroying the thickening ability of the cornstarch. Voilà! Chocolate soup!

In order to prevent this from happening, *the egg yolk–chocolate mixture must always be brought to a simmer,* or better yet a low boil, and then cooked *for a full minute.* And don't worry. The cornstarch prevents the egg yolks from scrambling. *Easy solution—delicious pie!* ❞

LOTS OF CHOCOLATE

## Microwave in Minutes

### THE EASY WAY TO MELT CHOCOLATE

Without a doubt, the microwave is the easiest place to melt chocolate quickly without burning or curdling it, provided you follow these simple steps:

- Chop the chocolate into uniform pieces, about ¼ inch or so.
- Use a dry knife and cutting board—the tiniest drop of water will cause melting chocolate to tighten up (called seizing), look curdled, and become unusable.
- Put the chopped chocolate into a dry microwaveable bowl.
- Microwave on High in 15-second intervals, until the chocolate melts, stirring between each interval. Watch carefully! Chocolate that's melted in the microwave holds its shape even after melted. Just stir until smooth.

# CHOCOLATE BANANA CREAM PIE

*Prep* **20 MINUTES**    *Bake* **18 MINUTES + CHILLING**

*Refrigerated cookie dough makes quick work of the pie's crust for a delicious chocolate banana cream pie.*

| | |
|---|---|
| 1 | package (18 ounces) refrigerated chocolate morsels cookie bar dough, softened |
| 1¾ | cups milk |
| 1 | package (3.4 ounces) banana cream or vanilla instant pudding and pie filling mix |
| 2 | medium ripe bananas, sliced |
| 1 | cup frozen whipped topping, thawed |
| 3 | tablespoons chocolate syrup |
| 3 | tablespoons semisweet mini chocolate morsels |

**LET'S BEGIN** Preheat the oven to 350°F. Grease a 9-inch pie pan. Break apart 15 squares of the cookie bar dough and press onto the bottom and up the sides of the pan. (You will have 5 squares left. Refrigerate for future use, or bake and enjoy!) Bake for 18 to 24 minutes, until golden brown. Flatten down with the back of a spoon to form a pie crust. Cool completely on a wire rack.

**BEAT IT** Meanwhile, beat the milk and pudding mix according to package directions in a small bowl. Refrigerate for 5 minutes.

**ASSEMBLE** Spread 1 cup of the pudding mixture over the crust (save the remaining pudding for another use). Top the pudding with the bananas, then spread with the whipped topping. Refrigerate the pie for at least 1 hour, until set. Drizzle with the chocolate syrup, then sprinkle with the chocolate morsels.

*Makes 8 servings*

*Per serving: 375 calories, 5g protein, 70g carbohydrates, 14g fat, 6g saturated fat, 20mg cholesterol, 350mg sodium*

# Brownie Bottom Pudding Pie

*Prep* **20 minutes**   *Bake* **25 minutes + chilling**

- 4 ounces (4 squares) semisweet baking chocolate
- ¼ cup butter or margarine
- ¾ cup sugar
- 2 large eggs
- 1 teaspoon vanilla extract
- ½ cup all-purpose flour
- ½ cup chopped pecans
- 2½ cups cold milk
- 2 packages (6-serving size each) chocolate instant pudding and pie filling mix
- 1 container (8 ounces) frozen whipped topping, thawed
- Grated semisweet baking chocolate (optional)

*What a delicious idea! Two favorite chocolate treats—brownies and chocolate pudding—rolled into one fabulous dessert. Here store-bought chocolate pudding and whipped topping keep your kitchen time short and sweet.*

**LET'S BEGIN** Preheat the oven to 350°F. Grease a 9-inch pie pan. Place the chocolate and butter in a large microwaveable bowl and microwave on High for 2 minutes, or until the butter is melted. Stir until the chocolate is completely melted. Add the sugar, eggs, and vanilla and mix until well blended. Stir in the flour and pecans. Spread into the pan.

**INTO THE OVEN** Bake for 25 minutes, or until a wooden toothpick inserted in the center comes out with fudgy crumbs (do not overbake). Cool completely on a wire rack.

**FILL & CHILL** Meanwhile, pour the milk into a large bowl. Add the pudding mix and whisk for 2 minutes. Let stand 2 minutes. Spread the pudding mixture over the crust. Top with the whipped topping and sprinkle with grated chocolate, if you wish. Refrigerate until ready to serve.

*Makes 10 servings*

*Per serving: 410 calories, 6g protein, 57g carbohydrates, 19g total fat, 11g saturated fat, 60mg cholesterol, 430mg sodium*

# White Chocolate Coconut Cream Pie

*Prep* **45 minutes**   *Bake* **10 minutes + chilling**

- 1½ cups sweetened flaked coconut
- 5 tablespoons butter or margarine, melted
- ½ cup graham cracker crumbs
- 6 ounces (6 squares) white baking chocolate
- 1¾ cups half-and-half
- 1 package (4-serving size) coconut cream instant pudding and pie filling mix
- 1½ cups heavy cream

*Take a trip to a tropical island with this tempting pie. Both the crust and the filling are laden with coconut, so you are sure to get lots of rich coconut flavor in every bite. If you like, sprinkle the whipped cream topping with a border of toasted coconut for an even more coconuty taste.*

**LET'S BEGIN** Preheat the oven to 350°F. Combine 1 cup coconut, 4 tablespoons butter, and the graham cracker crumbs in a 9-inch pie pan, until the crumbs are evenly moistened. Press the crumb mixture onto the bottom and up the sides of the pan. Bake for 10 minutes. Meanwhile, place 3 squares of the chocolate and the remaining 1 tablespoon butter in a small microwaveable bowl and microwave on High for 1½ minutes. Stir until the chocolate is completely melted. Spread onto the bottom of the crust. Refrigerate 15 minutes, or until the chocolate is firm.

**FILL & CHILL** Pour the half-and-half into a large bowl. Add the pudding mix and the remaining ½ cup coconut. Whisk for 2 minutes. Spoon into the crust. Refrigerate 30 minutes, or until beginning to firm. Meanwhile, place the remaining 3 squares chocolate and ¼ cup of the cream in a large microwaveable bowl and microwave on High for 2 minutes. Stir until the chocolate is completely melted. Cool, stirring occasionally, 20 minutes, or until the mixture is at room temperature.

**MAKE TOPPING** Beat the remaining 1¼ cups cream in a large chilled bowl with an electric mixer on medium-high speed until medium peaks form. Gently stir half of the whipped cream into the chocolate mixture until well blended. Gently stir in the remaining whipped cream. Spoon over the filling. Refrigerate at least 4 hours before serving.

*Makes 8 servings*
*Per serving: 600 calories, 6g protein, 40g carbohydrates, 47g fat, 31g saturated fat, 105mg cholesterol, 340mg sodium*

# Chocolate Pecan Pie

*Prep* **20 minutes**   Bake **1 hour**

- 1 (9-inch) unbaked pie shell
- 1 cup sugar
- ⅓ cup unsweetened cocoa
- 3 large eggs, slightly beaten
- 1 cup light corn syrup
- 1 tablespoon butter or margarine, melted
- 1 teaspoon vanilla extract
- 1 cup pecan halves
- 8 tablespoons sweetened whipped cream or whipped topping

*The only thing better than pecan pie is chocolate pecan pie. A generous amount of full-flavored cocoa makes this rendition especially chocolatey—yum! For easy slicing, be sure to let the pie cool completely.*

**LET'S BEGIN** Preheat the oven to 350°F. Prepare the pie crust (do not bake).

**MIX & FILL** Combine the sugar and cocoa in a medium bowl. Stir in the eggs, corn syrup, butter, and vanilla until well blended. Stir in the pecans. Pour into the pie shell.

**INTO THE OVEN** Bake for 1 hour, or until the center is set. Cool completely on a wire rack. Garnish with whipped cream.

Makes 8 servings

*Per serving: 490 calories, 6g protein, 70g carbohydrates, 24g fat, 6g saturated fat, 94mg cholesterol, 206mg sodium*

# Dark Chocolate Layered Cheesecake

*Prep* **30 minutes**   *Bake* **50 minutes + chilling**

## Chocolate Crumb Crust

- 1½ cups vanilla wafer crumbs (about 45 wafers)
- ½ cup confectioners' sugar
- ¼ cup unsweetened cocoa
- ¼ cup butter or margarine, melted

## Filling

- 1 package (12 ounces) dark chocolate chips
- 3 packages (8 ounces each) cream cheese, softened
- ¾ cup granulated sugar
- 4 large eggs
- ¼ cup heavy cream
- 2 teaspoons vanilla extract
- ¼ teaspoon salt
- ½ teaspoon vegetable shortening (do not use butter, margarine, spreads, or oil)

*Turn cookies into crumbs fast by breaking them up into coarse chunks, then pulsing them in a food processor.*

**LET'S BEGIN** To make the chocolate crumb crust, toss all the ingredients in a medium bowl until moistened. Press the mixture onto the bottom and 1½ inches up the side of a 9-inch springform pan. Preheat the oven to 350°F. To make the filling, set aside 2 tablespoons of the chocolate chips. Place the remaining chips in a large microwaveable bowl and microwave on High for 1½ minutes. Stir until the chocolate is melted. Set aside.

**MAKE LAYERS** Beat the cream cheese and granulated sugar in a large bowl with an electric mixer on medium-high speed until smooth. Beat in the eggs, then the cream, vanilla, and salt. With a rubber spatula, fold 1½ cups of the cheesecake batter into the melted chocolate. Spread 2 cups of the chocolate mixture onto the crust. Blend another 2 cups of the cheesecake batter into the remaining chocolate mixture. Spread 2 cups of the mixture over the first layer. Stir the remaining cheesecake batter into the remaining chocolate mixture and spread over the second layer.

**INTO THE OVEN** Bake for 50 to 55 minutes, until the center is almost set. Transfer the cheesecake to a wire rack. With a knife, immediately loosen the cake from the sides of the pan. Cool to room temperature. Microwave the reserved 2 tablespoons chocolate chips and the shortening in a small microwaveable bowl on High for 30 seconds and stir until the chocolate is melted. Drizzle the chocolate mixture over the top of the cheesecake. Cover and refrigerate at least several hours, until thoroughly chilled.

*Makes 10 servings*
*Per serving: 709 calories, 11g protein, 64g carbohydrates, 49g fat, 27g saturated fat, 181mg cholesterol, 411mg sodium*

# Easy Fudge Cake with Buttercream Frosting

*Prep* **30 minutes**   *Bake* **30 minutes**

- 2½ cups all-purpose flour
- 1¼ teaspoons baking soda
- 1 cup packed light brown sugar
- 1 cup granulated sugar
- ⅔ cup butter or margarine, softened
- 3 squares (3 ounces) unsweetened baking chocolate, melted and cooled
- ½ teaspoon salt
- 2 large eggs
- 1 teaspoon vanilla extract
- 1¼ cups cold water
- Buttercream Frosting (see recipe)

*Practically everyone loves chocolate—and this fudge cake is the best! The heavenly combination comes from using cocoa and both light brown sugar and granulated sugar in the cake . . . then a creamy buttercream frosting made with confectioners' sugar to top it all off. Even if you've never baked a cake before, you'll be able to make this fabulous creation—with confidence!*

**LET'S BEGIN** Preheat the oven to 350°F. Grease and flour two 9-inch round cake pans. Line the bottoms of the pans with waxed or parchment paper. Grease the paper. Combine the flour and baking soda in a small bowl. Beat the next 5 ingredients in a large bowl with an electric mixer on medium-high speed until light and fluffy. Add the eggs and vanilla. Beat 1 to 2 minutes until well mixed. Add the flour mixture alternately with the water, beginning and ending with the flour mixture and blending well after each addition. Pour the batter into the pans.

**INTO THE OVEN** Bake for 30 to 35 minutes, until the cake springs back when lightly touched. Cool the cakes in the pans for 10 minutes. Unmold onto wire racks and cool completely. Meanwhile, make the Buttercream Frosting and use it to fill and frost the cake.

## Buttercream Frosting

*Combine one 16-ounce package confectioners' sugar, ½ cup softened butter or margarine, 3 tablespoons milk, and 1 teaspon vanilla extract in a large bowl with an electric mixer on low speed. Increase the speed to medium and beat 1 to 2 minutes, until creamy. Add more milk, if necessary, until the frosting is spreadable.*

> *Makes 12 servings*
> Per serving: 595 calories, 5g protein, 94g carbohydrates, 24g fat, 12g saturated fat, 86mg cholesterol, 386mg sodium

# Black Forest Cake

*Prep* **10 MINUTES**   *Bake* **40 MINUTES + COOLING**

- 1 package (18.25 ounces) chocolate cake mix
- 1 can (21 ounces) cherry pie filling
- 2 large eggs
- 1 teaspoon almond extract
- 1 teaspoon vanilla extract
- 1 package (6 ounces) semisweet chocolate chips

*Desserts that contain chocolate and cherries are given the name Black Forest, after the region in Germany where Black Forest Cake originated. The mix of almond and vanilla extracts makes this one especially flavorful.*

**LET'S BEGIN** Preheat the oven to 350°F. Grease and flour a 13 × 9-inch baking pan.

**MIX IT UP** Combine the first 5 ingredients in a large bowl with an electric mixer on low speed. Increase the speed to medium and beat for 2 minutes. Fold in the chocolate chips. Pour the batter into the pan.

**INTO THE OVEN** Bake for 40 to 45 minutes, until a wooden toothpick inserted in the center comes out clean. Cool in the pan for 15 minutes. Invert the cake onto a wire rack and remove the pan. Invert again, right side up, and cool completely on the rack. Cut into squares.

*Makes 15 servings*
*Per serving: 250 calories, 3g protein, 47g carbohydrates, 7g fat, 3g saturated fat, 28mg cholesterol, 232mg sodium*

---

## Food Facts

### THANK GERMANY FOR THE BLACK FOREST CAKE!

The facts are hazy. But it has been hinted that the now-famous Black Forest Cake was created in Berlin around the 1930s. Others say it comes from Swabia in Germany's Black Forest region. Whatever its origin, this cake carries an authentic German name: Schwarzwalder Kirschtorte. It made its grand entrance onto dessert menus throughout the last half of the 20th century in Britain, the United States, and probably other countries too. And it remains a grand favorite today.

This confection typically makes a regal appearance whenever it's served. There are layers and layers of deep rich chocolate cake, with mounds of whipped cream and plenty of sweetened sour cherries separating each layer. To make it even more elegant, the layers are usually sprinkled generously with kirsch (the German cherry brandy), then the whole confection is frosted with sweetened whipped cream and decorated with plenty of chocolate curls. Divine!

# Heritage Chocolate Cake

*Prep* **35 minutes**  *Bake* **30 minutes + cooling**

- 2 cups all-purpose flour
- ½ cup unsweetened cocoa
- 1 teaspoon baking powder
- ¾ teaspoon baking soda
- ½ teaspoon salt
- ⅔ cup butter or margarine, softened
- 1¾ cups sugar
- 3 large eggs
- 1 teaspoon vanilla extract
- 1½ cups buttermilk or sour milk (see page 110)
- Chocolate Fudge Frosting (see recipe)

Sometimes doing a little bit of prep work ahead makes the baking go so much more smoothly and quickly. Measure the cake's dry ingredients into a resealable plastic bag 1 or even 2 days before you bake. You'll be surprised at how much time you save.

**LET'S BEGIN** Preheat the oven to 350°F. Grease and flour two 9-inch round cake pans.

**MIX IT UP** Combine the flour, cocoa, baking powder, baking soda, and salt in a medium bowl. Beat the butter, sugar, eggs, and vanilla in a large bowl with an electric mixer until light and fluffy. Add the flour mixture alternately with the buttermilk, beginning and ending with the flour mixture and beating just until smooth. Pour the batter into the pans.

**BAKE & FROST** Bake for 30 to 35 minutes, until a wooden toothpick inserted in the center comes out clean. Cool the cakes in the pans for 10 minutes. Unmold onto wire racks and cool completely. Meanwhile, make the Chocolate Fudge Frosting. To assemble, place 1 cake on a serving plate and frost the top. Place the remaining cake over the frosting and frost the top and sides.

## Chocolate Fudge Frosting

Melt ⅓ cup butter or margarine in a small saucepan over low heat. Stir in ⅓ cup unsweetened cocoa until smooth and slightly thickened. Pour into a medium bowl and cool completely. Using an electric mixer on high speed, beat in 2⅔ cups confectioners' sugar alternately with ⅓ cup milk mixed with 1 teaspoon vanilla extract, until of spreading consistency. Makes about 2 cups frosting.

*Makes 8 servings*

*Per serving: 720 calories, 9g protein, 113g carbohydrates, 28g fat, 14g saturated fat, 147mg cholesterol, 548mg sodium*

# Special Dark Picnic Cake

*Prep* **25 minutes**   *Bake* **35 minutes**

1 cup dark chocolate chips
¼ cup butter or margarine
1⅓ cups boiling water
2⅓ cups all-purpose flour
1¼ cups sugar
½ cup sour cream
2 large eggs
2 teaspoons baking soda
1 teaspoon vanilla extract
½ teaspoon salt
**Dark Frosting (see recipe)**

A double dose of dark chocolate chips makes this iced cake fabulous. The cake is super easy, as the butter doesn't get creamed. And baking it in a rectangular baking pan makes it nice and portable—just like the title suggests.

**LET'S BEGIN** Preheat the oven to 350°F. Grease and flour a 13 × 9-inch baking pan.

**MIX IT UP** Combine the chocolate chips, butter, and the boiling water in a large bowl. Stir until the chocolate is melted and the mixture is blended. Gradually beat in the flour, sugar, sour cream, eggs, baking soda, vanilla, and salt with an electric mixer on low speed. Increase the speed to medium and beat until smooth. Pour the batter into the pan.

**BAKE & FROST** Bake for 35 to 40 minutes, until a wooden toothpick inserted in the center comes out clean. Transfer to a wire rack and cool completely. Make the Dark Frosting and use to frost the top of the cake.

## Dark Frosting

Place 1 cup dark chocolate chips and ¼ cup butter or margarine in a medium microwaveable bowl and microwave on High for 1 minute. Stir until the chocolate is melted and the mixture is smooth. (If necessary, microwave an additional 15 seconds at a time, stirring after each heating.) Gradually beat in 1½ cups confectioners' sugar, ¼ cup milk, and ½ teaspoon vanilla extract with an electric mixer until smooth. If necessary, refrigerate the frosting for 5 to 10 minutes, until it's of desired spreading consistency. Makes about 1⅔ cups frosting.

**Makes 12 servings**
Per serving: 470 calories, 5g protein, 72g carbohydrates, 20g fat, 11g saturated fat, 61mg cholesterol, 387mg sodium

# Chocolate Espresso Fudge Cake

*Prep* **30 minutes**   *Bake* **50 minutes + chilling**

## CAKE

- 1½ cups butter, cut up
- ¾ cup granulated sugar
- ¾ cup water
- 1 tablespoon vanilla extract
- 2½ teaspoons instant espresso or 1½ tablespoons instant coffee
- 9 ounces semisweet chocolate, chopped
- 3 ounces unsweetened chocolate, chopped
- 6 large eggs, lightly beaten

## RASPBERRY SAUCE

- 2 packages (10 ounces each) frozen raspberries in syrup, thawed

## VANILLA WHIPPED CREAM

- 1 cup heavy cream
- ½ cup confectioners' sugar
- 2 teaspoons vanilla extract

*Here the best-ever flourless chocolate cake is served with an easy raspberry sauce and gently whipped cream. Absolutely fabulous!*

**LET'S BEGIN** Preheat the oven to 350°F. Coat a 9-inch springform pan with nonstick cooking spray. Line the bottom with waxed or parchment paper. Wrap the outside of the pan with foil. To make the cake, bring the first 5 ingredients to a boil in a large saucepan, then remove from the heat. Stir in the chocolates, until melted. Cool slightly, then whisk in the eggs until blended. Pour the batter into the pan.

**BAKE & CHILL** Place the springform pan in a larger baking pan. Place the baking pan on the oven rack. Carefully pour enough hot water into the baking pan to reach halfway up the side of the springform pan. Bake for 50 minutes, until set and a wooden toothpick inserted in the center comes out with a few moist crumbs attached. Remove the springform pan from the water bath. Transfer to a wire rack and cool. Cover and refrigerate at least 8 hours.

**UNMOLD & SERVE** Dip the bottom of the springform pan in a larger pan of hot water for 15 seconds. Run a sharp knife around the edge to loosen the cake and remove the springform side of the pan. Invert the cake onto the wire rack and remove the bottom of the pan and the paper. Invert again, right side up, onto a serving plate. To make the raspberry sauce, puree the raspberries and syrup in a food processor or blender. Strain through a fine sieve into a bowl. Discard the seeds. To make the vanilla whipped cream, beat the cream in a large bowl with an electric mixer on medium-high speed until soft peaks form. Gradually beat in the confectioners' sugar and vanilla and beat until stiff. Cut the cake into wedges and drizzle with the raspberry sauce. Top each serving with a scoop of whipped cream.

*Makes 16 servings*

*Per serving: 460 calories, 5g protein, 39g carbohydrates, 33g fat, 18g saturated fat, 148mg cholesterol, 172mg sodium*

Candy 'n' Balloon Birthday Cake, page 70

# For the Kids

What's more fitting than a dinosaur in the shape of a scrumptious cake to wish your child a happy birthday? Or some rainy afternoon, let the kids help you build a castle out of cake instead of wet sand. Another day, let their little hands help you turn brownies into a Mud Puddle Cake or a Graveyard Pizza. The fun goes on and on. There are ways to create a colorful butterfly and a happy bunny out of cake, plus terrific ideas for decorating cakes when you're pressed for time. Start dreaming up your own cake creations with your kids and enter them into the next county fair or take them to the next birthday party. You just might bring home a blue ribbon!

# Brownie Mud Puddle Cake

*Prep* **20 minutes**   *Bake* **25 minutes + decorating**

- 4 ounces (4 squares) unsweetened baking chocolate
- ¾ cup butter or margarine
- 2 cups sugar
- 3 large eggs
- 1 teaspoon vanilla extract
- 1 cup all-purpose flour
- 1 cup cold milk
- 1 package (3 ounces) chocolate instant pudding and pie filling mix
- 10 chocolate sandwich cookies, crushed (about ½ cup)
- Easy Marshmallow Snails (optional, see recipe)

*This is the perfect chocolate dessert treat for a child's party. A brownie "crust" is topped with a chocolate pudding "puddle," sprinkled with chocolate cookie "dirt," and decorated with fruit gelatin "snails." Let the fun begin!*

**LET'S BEGIN** Preheat the oven to 350°F. Grease a 12-inch pizza pan. Place the chocolate and butter in a large microwaveable bowl and microwave on High for 2 minutes, or until the butter is melted. Stir until the chocolate is completely melted. Stir in the sugar. Blend in the eggs and vanilla. Add the flour and mix well. Spread into the pan.

**INTO THE OVEN** Bake for 25 to 30 minutes, until a wooden toothpick inserted in the center comes out with fudgy crumbs. (Do not overbake.) Cool in the pan on a wire rack.

**TOPPING** Pour the milk into a large bowl. Add the pudding mix and whisk for 2 minutes. Spread over the brownie, leaving a 1-inch border around the edge. Sprinkle with crushed cookies to resemble dirt. Cut into 16 wedges to serve. Decorate with the Easy Marshmallow Snails, if you like.

## Easy Marshmallow Snails

*Coat a 9-inch square baking pan with nonstick cooking spray. Combine a package of gelatin (any flavor) and ½ cup warm water in a medium microwaveable bowl. Microwave on High 1½ minutes, then stir until the gelatin is completely dissolved. Measure out 1¾ cups mini marshmallows and set aside 12 of them. Add the remaining marshmallows to the gelatin and stir until well blended. Microwave on High 1 minute, or until the marshmallows are partially melted. Whisk until the marshmallows are completely melted. Pour into the pan. Refrigerate for 45 minutes, or until set. Run a sharp knife around the edges of the pan to loosen the gelatin layer from the pan. Starting at one end, roll up the gelatin layer tightly.*

Cut into twelve ¾-inch-thick strips. Unroll each strip about 1 inch. Stand 1 of the reserved marshmallows on the unrolled portion of each spiral for the "snail's body," securing it with prepared vanilla frosting (you will need about ¼ cup total). Starting with 24 inches of red shoestring licorice, cut twenty-four 1-inch pieces. Insert 2 pieces of licorice into each marshmallow for "antennae," securing with the frosting, if you like.

### Makes 16 servings

Per serving (without marshmallow snails): 320 calories, 4g protein, 45g carbohydrates, 15g fat, 8g saturated fat, 65mg cholesterol, 250mg sodium

# Sand Castle Cake

Prep **20 MINUTES**  Bake **ABOUT 27 MINUTES + DECORATING**

| | |
|---|---|
| 1 | 8-inch square white cake (prepared from a cake mix) |
| 1 | tub (16 ounces) prepared vanilla frosting |
| 1 | cup turbinado sugar |
| 6 | whole graham crackers |
| 4 | cake ice cream cones |

Blue food coloring

| | |
|---|---|
| 2 | cups gummy fish, jelly beans, or gumdrops |

Create a "Day at the Beach" theme for a children's party using this easy-to-make cake as the centerpiece. You'll be delighted to see that the sugar really does look like sand! You and your child can create the cake the day before the party or make it a fun project for several kids to do together. Note: Leftover batter from the cake mix can be used to make cupcakes.

**LET'S BEGIN** Cover a 12-inch cardboard circle with foil, attaching the underside with tape. Arrange the cake in the center of the circle. Spread about one-third of the frosting over the top and sides of the cake. Coat all sides of the cake with some of the sugar. (Working over a sheet of waxed paper, brush away any excess sugar from the circle and reserve.)

**MAKE PILLARS** Break the graham crackers along the perforations into 12 rectangles. Frost and coat both sides of the crackers with sugar except for the bottom half on one side. Gently press the unfrosted sides of the crackers onto each side of the cake, 3 crackers per side, to resemble the stone "pillars" of a castle.

**FINISHING TOUCHES** Lightly frost the outside of the ice cream cones, coat them with the remaining sugar, and set aside. In a bowl, tint the remaining frosting with the food coloring. Spread the blue frosting on the cardboard circle from where the cake sits all the way to the edge, to create the castle's "moat." Place gummy fish on top. Attach an ice cream cone, upright, at each corner of the "castle" to make the "turrets." Fill the cones with jelly beans or gumdrops. Refrigerate the cake until ready to serve.

*Makes 12 servings*

*Per serving: 422 calories, 2g protein, 78g carbohydrates, 11g fat, 2g saturated fat, 0mg cholesterol, 263mg sodium*

# Butterfly Cake

Prep **20 MINUTES**    Bake **ABOUT 27 MINUTES + DECORATING**

*Fruit jams make a bright-colored butterfly-shaped dessert that resembles intricate stained glass, and kids can do all the design work themselves. Avoid preserves that contain pieces of fruit—they won't give a smooth, finished surface. Note: Leftover cake batter can be used for cupcakes.*

- 1    8-inch round white or yellow cake (prepared from a cake mix)
- 1    cup prepared vanilla frosting
- 1    cup turbinado sugar
-      Assorted jams, such as grape, apricot, or strawberry
- 2    pieces (1-inch each) black shoestring licorice

**LET'S BEGIN** Cut the cake in half with a serrated knife. Put the rounded sides back to back on a serving tray or large plate, and cut out a small semicircle on the flat side of each half to create the wings. Generously frost the sides of the cake with the vanilla frosting. Coat the frosted sides with some of the sugar. (Working over a sheet of waxed paper, brush away any excess sugar from the tray and reserve.)

**DECORATE** With a butter knife, randomly place about 1 teaspoon of each variety of jam, alternating colors, on the top of the cake. Spread in small patches, with spaces inbetween, to resemble the random look of a stained glass window. Place the remaining sugar in a resealable plastic bag and snip a small hole at one corner. Drizzle the sugar in the spaces between the jam patches. For the butterfly's antenna, insert the licorice pieces at the top of the cake where the two semicircles meet.

> Makes 12 servings
> *Per serving: 280 calories, 1g protein, 50g carbohydrates, 8g fat, 2g saturated fat, 0mg cholesterol, 190mg sodium*

---

**Food Facts**

### BIRTHDAY CAKE TRADITIONS

The tradition of celebrating birthdays dates almost as far back as human history. Early on, it was believed that evil spirits were more dangerous after a person experienced a change in life, such as a birthday. As a result, birthdays became happy occasions where the person of honor was surrounded with merriment to protect them from such evil.

It is thought that cake became part of the celebratory tradition with the Greeks, who took cake (whose roundness represented the full moon) to the temple of the goddess of the moon as an offering. Others believe that the tradition began in Germany, where a bread was baked in the shape of the baby Jesus's swaddling clothes.

In England, ever since medieval times, birthday cakes have been baked with symbolic objects (such as coins) inside. Eventually, the idea of setting out one candle for each year of life became the most popular way to honor the day, and it remains so today.

# Candy 'n' Balloon Birthday Cake

*Prep* **30 minutes**   *Bake* **27 minutes + decorating**

- **2** 9-inch round confetti, yellow, or white cakes (prepared from a cake mix)

### ICING

- **1** package (2 pounds) confectioners' sugar, sifted
- **¾** cup half-and-half
- **1** teaspoon almond extract

Red, yellow, and blue food coloring

### GARNISH

- **2** brightly colored or white plastic 9-inch plates

Blue Easter grass or colored shredded paper

Yellow curling ribbon

Inflated balloons

Party noisemakers

Gumballs

*Why spend money on a store-bought birthday cake when you can make one that is quick and easy and you know will be delicious? Have fun with the garnishes—it will guarantee a festive mood for the party.*

**LET'S BEGIN** To make the icing, beat the sugar, half-and-half, and almond extract in a large bowl with an electric mixer on low speed, scraping the bowl often, 1 to 2 minutes, until well mixed.

**TINT & DECORATE** Reserve 1 cup of the icing and set aside. Frost the tops and sides of the cakes with the remaining icing. Divide the reserved icing among 3 small bowls. Tint each with the red, yellow, and blue food coloring to make bright colors. Fill 3 small resealable plastic bags with one colored icing each. Cut off 1 corner of each bag with scissors. Decorate each cake by piping the tinted icings in polka dots or whimsical geometric designs.

**FINISHING TOUCHES** Place each decorated cake in the center of a plastic plate and cut off the excess plate. Spread the Easter grass over a 20-inch flat tray or foil-covered cardboard. Arrange the cakes on the tray so they appear to be floating in the air. For the balloon strings, insert ribbons into the bottom of each cake. Arrange the balloons, noisemakers, and gumballs around the cakes.

*Makes 16 servings*

Per serving: 460 calories, 3g protein, 84g carbohydrates, 14g fat, 4g saturated fat, 45mg cholesterol, 155mg sodium

# Jack O' Lantern

*Prep* **25 minutes**   *Bake* **22 minutes**

- ¾ cup butter or margarine, melted
- 1½ cups sugar
- 1½ teaspoons vanilla extract
- 3 large eggs
- ¾ cup all-purpose flour
- ½ cup unsweetened cocoa
- ½ teaspoon baking powder
- ¼ teaspoon salt
- 1 tub (16 ounces) prepared vanilla frosting

Yellow and red food colors

Assorted candies (optional): butterscotch baking chips, red string licorice, black licorice bits, English toffee bits, and gumdrops

*Jack has never looked or tasted so good! Let the kids help decorate him. He's now ready for that Halloween party!*

**LET'S BEGIN** Preheat the oven to 350°F. Grease a 12-inch pizza pan. Beat the melted butter, sugar, and vanilla in a large bowl with a spoon. Beat in the eggs. Stir in the next 4 ingredients and beat until well blended.

**BAKE** Spread the batter in the pan. Bake for 20 to 22 minutes, or until the top springs back when lightly touched in the center. Cool completely on a wire rack.

**DECORATE** Stir the frosting and food colors together in a medium bowl for the desired shade of orange, making certain that the color is evenly distributed. Frost the brownie and decorate with the candies to resemble a jack-o-lantern. Use butterscotch chips for his eyes, red string licorice for his eyebrows and mouth, black licorice bits for his teeth, English toffee bits for his nose, and a green gumdrop for his stem.

*Makes 12 brownies*

*Per brownie (decorated): 440 calories, 3g protein, 61g carbohydrate, 21g total fat, 9g saturated fat, 86mg cholesterol, 247mg sodium*

---

## Baking Basics

### REMOVING THE CAKE FROM THE PAN—WITHOUT LOSING A CRUMB!

When you remove a cake from the oven, it's very hot and very fragile. If it's a foam-type cake, such as sponge, chiffon, or angel food, turn it upside down immediately and let it cool completely before trying to remove it from the pan.

Let all other cakes rest for 10 minutes in their pan before being removed. Here are more tips for best results:

- Run a small, thin knife all around the sides of the pan to ensure the cake has been released. Then, holding one cake rack on top of the cake and a second one underneath, turn the cake upside down, letting the cake gently slip out of the pan onto the top rack. If it needs a little help, shake it ever so gently.

- If a cake refuses to come out of its pan, set the pan in a sink filled with a little hot water and let it stand for about 2 minutes to warm it briefly. Or pop it into the still-warm oven to briefly warm it.

# Dinosaur Birthday Cake

Prep **20 minutes**    Bake **27 minutes + decorating**

| | |
|---|---|
| 1 | 13 × 9-inch cake, any flavor (prepared from a cake mix) |
| 1 | container (8 ounces) frozen whipped topping, thawed |
| 3 | to 4 drops each red and blue food coloring |
| 1 | roll five-flavor roll candy or gummies (14 candies) |
| ¼ | cup assorted small candy balls |

*This cake works beautifully with any favorite cake mix flavor you like. You can even bake it a day ahead. Just be sure to give the whipped topping enough time to thaw.*

**LET'S BEGIN** Transfer the cooled cake to a cutting board and cut into pieces as shown in the Dinosaur Illustration (see below).

**ASSEMBLE & DECORATE** Tint the whipped topping with the red and blue food coloring to make it purple. Using a small amount of whipped topping to hold pieces together, arrange the cake on a serving tray so that "B" attaches to "A" and forms the head of the dinosaur, "C" attaches to "A" to form the tail, and the 4 "D" pieces are placed along the back.

**FROST IT** Frost the cake with the remaining whipped topping. Decorate with the candies.

*Makes 10 servings*

Per serving: 240 calories, 2g protein, 41g carbohydrates, 8g fat, 5g saturated fat, 0mg cholesterol, 240mg sodium

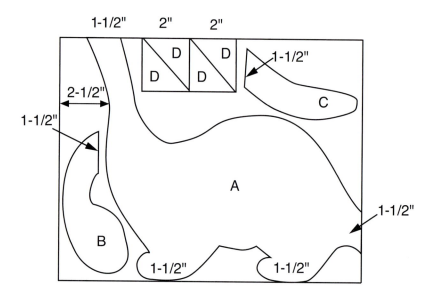

72   BLUE RIBBON CAKES & PIES

# GRAVEYARD PIZZA

*Prep* **15 MINUTES**     *Bake* **21 MINUTES + DECORATING**

- 16    Halloween chocolate sandwich cookies
- 1     package (19.5 ounces) brownie mix
- 1¼   cups mini marshmallows
- White decorating icing
- Assorted Halloween candies (gummy worms or bugs)

*The perfect cake for celebrating Halloween! Be sure to let little helping hands assist on this baking project; it will make it so much more fun.*

**LET'S BEGIN** Preheat the oven to 350°F. Grease a 14-inch pizza pan. Chop 8 of the cookies and set aside.

**INTO THE OVEN** Prepare the brownie mix according to package directions and spread the batter into the pan. Bake for 18 to 20 minutes, until a wooden toothpick inserted in the center comes out clean. Immediately sprinkle the marshmallows over the top of the hot brownie and bake 3 to 5 minutes longer, until the marshmallows are lightly browned. Immediately sprinkle the chopped cookies over the marshmallows. Cool on a wire rack.

**FINISHING TOUCHES** Decorate the remaining 8 cookies with the icing to resemble tombstones. Stand the "tombstones" around the brownie, pressing them gently into it. Decorate with the assorted candies as desired.

*Makes 16 servings*

*Per serving: 330 calories, 3g protein, 48g carbohydrates, 14g fat, 3g saturated fat, 25mg cholesterol, 190mg sodium*

---

## Time Savers

### 4 FAST WAYS TO DECORATE BIRTHDAY CAKES

Sure, it's great if you have time to decorate a birthday cake the old-fashioned way—but if your time is tight, there are still ways to get the birthday cake ready for the party.

**Candy Land** Ice the cake with prepared or homemade frosting, finishing it with deep swirls. Shower the top with mini milk chocolate M&M baking bits in all colors.

**Wheels of Chocolate** Ice the cake with chocolate frosting, finishing off the top with deep swirls. Make a border of vanilla-filled chocolate sandwich cookies around the edge, overlapping them slightly. Mound the center with unwrapped chocolate candy kisses.

**Favorite Things** Ice the cake with vanilla buttercream. Write the child's birthday wishes (his favorite things, such as "swimming," "camping," "ice cream," etc.) using different colors of jelly beans.

**Gumdrop Art** Ice the cake with chocolate frosting (either prepared or homemade). Using a wooden toothpick, draw an outline of a favorite object such as a butterfly or a kite. Using different colored gumdrops, outline the object by standing up the gumdrops. Decorate the sides of the cake with extra gumdrops.

FOR THE KIDS

## *SuperQuick*
# HONEY-ALMOND SWEET PIZZA

Prep **10 MINUTES**    Bake **11 MINUTES + STANDING**

| | |
|---|---|
| ¼ | cup honey |
| | Large pinch ground cinnamon |
| 1 | tube (10 ounces) refrigerated pizza dough |
| 2 | tablespoons butter, melted |
| ¼ | cup slivered almonds, lightly toasted |

*Pizza for dessert is such a clever—and easy—idea the kids will love.*

**LET'S BEGIN** Preheat the oven to 450°F. Combine the honey and the cinnamon in a small bowl. Set aside.

**INTO THE OVEN** Shape the pizza dough according to package directions for a thin-crusted pizza and brush the surface with the melted butter. Bake for 5 minutes. Brush the honey mixture over the partially baked pizza shell and sprinkle with the almonds. Bake 6 minutes longer, or until the crust is golden. Transfer to a cutting board and let stand 5 minutes. Cut into 12 wedges. Serve warm or at room temperature.

**Makes 6 servings**

*Per serving: 230 calories, 5g protein, 35g carbohydrates, 9g fat, 3g saturated fat, 11mg cholesterol, 290mg sodium*

# S'MORE COOKIE BARS

Prep **15 MINUTES**    Bake **30 MINUTES**

| | |
|---|---|
| 1⅓ | cups all-purpose flour |
| ¾ | cup graham cracker crumbs |
| 1 | teaspoon baking powder |
| ¼ | teaspoon salt |
| ½ | cup butter or margarine, softened |
| ¾ | cup sugar |
| 1 | large egg |
| 1 | teaspoon vanilla extract |
| 4 | bars (1.55 ounces each) milk chocolate |
| 1 | cup marshmallow creme |

*The only thing better than s'mores is s'mores cookie bars!*

**LET'S BEGIN** Preheat the oven to 350°F. Grease an 8-inch square baking pan. Combine the flour, graham cracker crumbs, baking powder, and salt in a medium bowl. Beat the butter and sugar in a large bowl with an electric mixer until light and fluffy. Beat in the egg and vanilla. Beat in the flour mixture just until blended. Press half the dough into the pan. Arrange the chocolate bars over the dough, breaking as needed to fit. Spread the top with the marshmallow creme. Top with bits of remaining dough and press gently.

**INTO THE OVEN** Bake for 30 to 35 minutes, until lightly browned. Cool completely on a wire rack. Cut into 16 bars.

**Makes 16 bars**

*Per bar: 270 calories, 3g protein, 41g carbohydrates, 10g fat, 5g saturated fat, 32mg cholesterol, 130mg sodium*

# Bunny Cake

*Prep* **20 minutes**   *Bake* **about 27 minutes + decorating**

- 2    8- or 9-inch round cakes, any flavor (prepared from a cake mix)
- 1    tub (16 ounces) prepared vanilla frosting
- 1    package (7 ounces) flaked sweetened coconut
- 2    teaspoons water
- 2    drops green food coloring
- 2    drops red food coloring
- Red shoestring licorice, 2 green jelly beans, 1 pink jelly bean, and pink and yellow candy-coated chocolate candies

*Hop on in to your kitchen and bake this fun cake for the little "bunnies" in your family.*

**LET'S BEGIN** Cut the cakes according to the diagram (see below). For easier frosting, freeze the pieces uncovered for 1 hour, if you like. Arrange the pieces on a large tray in a bunny shape as shown, attaching the pieces with a small amount of the frosting. Frost the top and sides of the pieces with the remaining frosting.

**DECORATE** Set aside ¼ cup coconut. Place ½ cup coconut in a plastic bag. Combine the green food coloring with 1 teaspoon water in a cup. Add to the coconut in the bag. Seal the bag and toss until the coconut is tinted green. Place the remaining coconut in another plastic bag. Combine the red food coloring with 1 teaspoon water in another cup, then add to that bag. Seal the bag and toss until the coconut is tinted pink. Sprinkle the bunny ears and face with the pink coconut. Sprinkle the bunny's tie with the green coconut. Sprinkle the inside of the bunny's ears with the reserved ¼ cup white coconut. Attach the licorice for the whiskers, the green jelly beans for the eyes, and the pink jelly bean for the nose. Decorate the tie with the pink and yellow candies.

*Makes 12 servings*

*Per serving: 520 calories, 4g protein, 74g carbohydrates, 23g total fat, 10g saturated fat, 55g cholesterol, 414mg sodium*

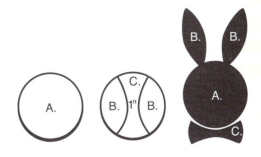

**FOR THE KIDS**

# Chocolate Chip Cookie Cake

*Prep* **20 minutes**   *Bake* **40 minutes + cooling**

- 2½ cups all-purpose flour
- 1½ cups granulated sugar
- ¾ cup milk
- ¾ cup butter, melted, or vegetable oil
- 4 large eggs
- 4 teaspoons vanilla extract
- 1 tablespoon baking powder
- ½ teaspoon salt
- ¾ cup semisweet chocolate mini chips

**GLAZE**

- ⅓ cup confectioners' sugar
- ⅓ cup water
- 1 tablespoon butter
- 2 teaspoons vanilla extract

*This cake will remind you of the best chocolate chip cookies you've ever had. We find that the easiest and quickest way to grease and flour a Bundt pan is to use the flour-and-oil spray that is found in the baking aisle in supermarkets.*

**LET'S BEGIN** Preheat the oven to 325°F. Generously grease and flour a 12-cup Bundt cake or fluted tube pan. Beat the first 8 ingredients in a large bowl with an electric mixer on low speed for 30 seconds. Scrape the sides of the bowl, increase the speed to medium, and beat for 3 minutes. Fold in the chocolate chips. Pour the batter into the pan.

**INTO THE OVEN** Bake for 40 to 50 minutes, until a wooden toothpick inserted in the center comes out clean. Transfer the cake to a wire rack. With tines of a fork, deeply pierce the cake at 1-inch intervals.

**GLAZE IT** Meanwhile, to make the glaze, bring all of the ingredients to a boil in a small saucepan. Reduce the heat and simmer for 1 minute. Spoon half the glaze over the hot cake. Let the cake stand for 10 minutes, then invert onto a serving plate. Spoon the remaining glaze over the cake. Cool completely.

*Makes 16 servings*

*Per serving: 327 calories, 5g protein, 43g carbohydrates, 15g fat, 7g saturated fat, 81mg cholesterol, 271mg sodium*

# Winter Wonderland Snowmen

Prep **15 minutes**   Bake **35 minutes + chilling**

- ¾ cup unsweetened cocoa or Dutch processed cocoa
- ½ teaspoon baking soda
- ⅔ cup butter or margarine, melted
- ½ cup boiling water
- 2 cups granulated sugar
- 2 large eggs
- 1 teaspoon vanilla extract
- 1½ cups all-purpose flour
- 1 package (10 ounces) peanut butter chips
- Confectioners' sugar
- Decorations: chocolate chips, unsalted peanuts, red decorator's icing

When it's snowing outside, and even if it's not, let the kids help you bake these smiling snowmen. The best part? They won't melt away because they're not made of snow! Instead, they're a rich brownie with yummy peanut butter chips throughout. So they're as delicious to eat as they are fun to make!

**LET'S BEGIN** Preheat the oven to 350°F. Line a 13 × 9-inch baking pan with foil and grease the foil.

**MIX & BLEND** Stir the cocoa and baking soda together in a large bowl, then stir in ⅓ cup of the melted butter. Add the boiling water and stir until the mixture thickens. Stir in the granulated sugar, eggs, vanilla, and the remaining ⅓ cup melted butter until smooth. Add the flour and stir until blended. Stir in the peanut butter chips. Pour into the pan.

**INTO THE OVEN** Bake for 35 to 40 minutes, or until the brownies begin to pull away from the sides of the foil. Cool completely in the pan on a wire rack. Cover and refrigerate for 2 hours, or until firm. Remove from the pan and remove the foil.

**DECORATE** Cut out snowmen with a snowman cookie cutter. Just before serving, sprinkle each snowman all over, except for his hat, with confectioners' sugar. Use 2 chocolate chips for his eyes, 3 peanuts for his buttons, and red icing for his mouth.

If you prefer not to decorate them, cut the brownie into 36 bars (2" × 1¼").

*Makes 12 large snowmen or 3 dozen bars*

Per snowman (decorated): 499 calories, 10g protein, 66g carbohydrate, 23g total fat, 14g saturated fat, 64mg cholesterol, 199mg sodium
Per bar (undecorated): 143 calories, 3g protein, 19g carbohydrate, 6g total fat, 4g saturated fat, 21mg cholesterol, 66mg sodium

# Peanutty Goober Cake

Prep **10 minutes**   Bake **40 minutes + cooling**

| | |
|---|---|
| 1 | package (18.25 ounces) yellow cake mix |
| 1 | cup creamy peanut butter |
| ½ | cup firmly packed light brown sugar |
| 1 | cup water |
| 3 | large eggs |
| ¼ | cup vegetable oil |
| 1 | package (6 ounces) peanut butter and milk chocolate morsels |
| 1 | package (7 ounces) milk chocolate–covered peanuts |

*An American-flavor tradition, the combination of peanuts and chocolate is simply a very clever way to add fun taste to an already delicious cake.*

**LET'S BEGIN** Preheat the oven to 350°F. Lightly grease a 13 × 9-inch baking pan.

**MIX IT UP** Beat the first 3 ingredients in a large bowl with an electric mixer on low speed until crumbly. Transfer ½ cup of the crumb mixture to a small bowl and set aside. Beat the water, eggs, and oil into the remaining crumb mixture until moistened. Increase the speed to high and beat for 2 minutes. Stir in ½ cup of the morsels. Pour into the prepared baking pan. Sprinkle the chocolate-covered peanuts, the remaining morsels, and the reserved crumb mixture over the batter.

**INTO THE OVEN** Bake for 40 to 45 minutes, until a wooden toothpick inserted in the center comes out clean. Cool completely on a wire rack.

*Makes 12 servings*

*Per serving: 567 calories, 13g protein, 62g carbohydrates, 31g fat, 9g saturated fat, 56mg cholesterol, 439mg sodium*

# DALMATIAN CUPCAKES

*Prep* **15 MINUTES**   *Bake* **15 MINUTES**

- 1 package (18.25 ounces) white cake mix
- ¼ cup vegetable oil
- 3 large eggs
- 1¼ cups water
- 1 package (12 ounces) semisweet chocolate mini morsels
- 1 tub (16 ounces) prepared vanilla frosting

*Rent 101 Dalmatians and enjoy these whimsical cupcakes at the same time.*

**LET'S BEGIN** Preheat the oven to 350°F. Grease twenty-four 2- to 3-inch muffin cups or line with paper liners.

**MIX IT UP** Beat the cake mix, oil, eggs, and water in a large bowl with an electric mixer on low speed for 1 minute. Scrape down the sides of the bowl with a rubber spatula, increase the speed to high, and beat for 1 minute. Stir in 1½ cups of the chocolate morsels. Spoon the batter into the muffin cups.

**INTO THE OVEN** Bake for 15 to 20 minutes, until a wooden toothpick inserted in the center comes out clean. Cool the cupcakes in the pans for 10 minutes. Remove the cupcakes onto wire racks and cool completely. Frost the cupcakes. Sprinkle the tops with the remaining ½ cup chocolate morsels.

*Makes 2 dozen cupcakes*

*Per cupcake: 545 calories, 5g protein, 77g carbohydrates, 26g fat, 8g saturated fat, 53mg cholesterol, 385mg sodium*

**FOR THE KIDS**   79

# CUPID'S CUPCAKES

*Prep* **10 MINUTES**   *Bake* **24 MINUTES + COOLING**

- 1 package (18.25 ounces) white cake mix
- 14 drops red food coloring

**PINK FROST ICING**
- 1 tub (16 ounces) prepared vanilla frosting
- 6 drops red food coloring

Tiny red heart candies (optional)

*Easy-to-use red food coloring makes these super-quick cupcakes just right for Valentine's Day.*

**LET'S BEGIN** Prepare the cake mix batter according to package directions. Transfer half the batter to another bowl. Tint half the batter with the food coloring.

**FILL & SWIRL** Line twenty-four 2- to 3-inch muffin cups with paper liners. Pour the plain batter into the muffin cups, filling them about two-thirds full. Top with the pink batter and swirl the batters with a small knife to marbleize.

**BAKE & FROST** Bake the cupcakes according to package directions. Cool in the pans for 10 minutes. Remove the cupcakes onto wire racks and cool completely. To make the Pink Frost Icing, combine the frosting and food coloring in a medium bowl, and stir until the color is evenly distributed. Frost the tops of the cupcakes with the icing. Decorate with heart candies, if you wish.

*Makes 2 dozen cupcakes*

*Per cupcake: 192 calories, 1g protein, 30g carbohydrates, 7g fat, 2g saturated fat, 0mg cholesterol, 176mg sodium*

## Baking Basics

### CUPCAKES FROM YOUR FAVORITE RECIPE

You have to make cupcakes for your child's class, and you'd like to use your favorite layer cake recipe. Will it work? Yes—almost any butter cake recipe can be made into cupcakes. Here's how:

| Your Recipe Makes | Number of Cupcakes |
| --- | --- |
| Two 8-inch round layers | 24 cupcakes |
| One 7 × 11-inch layer | 24 cupcakes |
| Two 9-inch round layers | 36 cupcakes |
| One 9 × 13-inch layer | 36 cupcakes |

Bake the cupcakes at 350°F for 15 to 20 minutes, until a wooden toothpick inserted in the center comes out clean.

*Holiday Fruited Pound Cake, page 101*

# For the Season

Whatever the season, 'tis time to bake a cake! Whenever Mom gets out her heart cake pan, you know it's either Valentine's Day or Dad's birthday. And when her Strawberry Rhubarb Custard Pie shows up for dessert, summer can't be far behind. Then, it'll soon be the season for those scrumptious fresh blueberry pies, peach pies, and fresh strawberry everything. Once the frost shows up on the pumpkins, you'll know that Mom's favorite apple pie will soon be coming out of the oven, followed by her spice cake another day. These delights are all here, waiting for you to head into the kitchen and start baking. Everyone loves a piece of homemade cake or a slice of fresh-from-the-oven pie!

# 'Tis Spring! Cheesecake

*Prep* **30 minutes**   *Bake* **55 minutes + chilling**

- 1½ cups chocolate graham cracker crumbs
- ¼ cup butter or margarine, melted
- 36 chocolate-covered butterfinger eggs
- 3 packages (8 ounces each) cream cheese, softened
- 1 cup sugar
- 1 tablespoon vanilla extract
- 3 large eggs

**TOPPING**

- 1 container (16 ounces) sour cream
- ¼ cup sugar
- 1 teaspoon vanilla extract

*Sweetened sour cream has become a time-honored way to top many a cheesecake. Sometimes it is used to mask the cracks that occasionally appear, but here it just adds an extra bit of sweet richness that complements the cake.*

**LET'S BEGIN** Preheat the oven to 350°F. Grease the bottom and sides of a 9-inch springform pan. Combine the graham cracker crumbs and butter in a medium bowl until the mixture is evenly moistened. Press onto the bottom of the pan. Freeze while making the filling.

**FILL IT** Reserve 12 butterfinger eggs to use for the garnish. Unwrap the remaining butterfinger eggs, cut into quarters, and set aside. Beat the cream cheese and sugar in a large bowl with an electric mixer at medium-high speed until fluffy. Beat in the vanilla. Add the eggs, one at a time, beating well after each addition. Sprinkle the cut-up butterfinger eggs over the bottom of the crust, leaving a ½-inch border. Pour the filling over the butterfinger eggs.

**INTO THE OVEN** Bake for 50 minutes, or until the center is set and the edges begin to crack. Meanwhile, to make the topping, combine all the ingredients in a medium bowl and mix well. When the cheesecake is done, transfer to a wire rack (keep the oven on). Let stand for 2 minutes. Spread the topping evenly over the surface of the cheesecake. Bake 5 minutes longer. Return the cheesecake to the wire rack and cool completely. Cover and refrigerate at least 6 hours or overnight. To serve, run a sharp knife around the edge to loosen the cheesecake and remove the springform side of the pan. Garnish each slice with 1 unwrapped butterfinger egg.

*Makes 12 servings*

*Per serving: 565 calories, 9g protein, 47g carbohydrates, 38g fat, 22g saturated fat, 143mg cholesterol, 333mg sodium*

# Strawberry Crown Tart

*Prep* **30 minutes**   *Bake* **30 minutes**

Pastry for a single-crust 9-inch pie

2 large eggs

⅓ cup sugar

1 tablespoon lemon juice

1 teaspoon grated lemon zest

½ teaspoon vanilla extract

½ cup all-purpose flour

3 tablespoons butter or margarine, melted and cooled

⅓ cup red currant jelly, melted

2 baskets (1 pint each) fresh strawberries, stemmed

*Brushing the pastry shell with currant jelly helps to keep it from turning soggy in the oven. Pick out uniform-sized strawberries for the top of the tart, then slice the remaining berries for the filling.*

**LET'S BEGIN** Preheat the oven to 425°F. Press the pastry dough into a 9-inch tart pan with a removable bottom. Prick all over with a fork. Bake for 10 to 12 minutes, just until the pastry begins to brown. Cool completely on a wire rack.

**FILL IT** Reduce the oven temperature to 375°F. Beat the eggs, sugar, lemon juice, lemon zest, and vanilla in a large bowl with an electric mixer until thick and lemon-colored, about 10 minutes. With a rubber spatula, gently fold one-third of the flour into the egg mixture, then fold in one-third of the butter. Continue folding, alternating the flour and butter, until all has been incorporated. (Do not overmix.) Brush the bottom of the tart shell with some of the jelly. Slice about half of the strawberries and arrange over the jelly. Pour the batter over the strawberries (it will not quite cover).

**INTO THE OVEN** Bake for 20 to 25 minutes, until golden and the filling is set. Cool completely on a wire rack. Remove the side of the tart pan. Arrange the remaining whole strawberries, stem ends down, on top of the tart. Brush with the remaining jelly.

*Makes 8 servings*

*Per serving: 282 calories, 4g protein, 38g carbohydrates, 13g fat, 5g saturated fat, 55mg cholesterol, 171 mg sodium*

# Strawberry Rhubarb Custard Pie

Prep **15 minutes**   Bake **40 minutes**

- 1¼ cups sugar
- ½ cup all-purpose flour
- 2 cups diced fresh rhubarb
- 1 cup sliced fresh strawberries + extra for garnish (optional)
- 1 (9-inch) unbaked deep-dish pie shell
- 4 large eggs
- ¼ cup low-fat or skim milk
- 1 teaspoon almond extract

All good cooks know that foods that ripen at the same time usually taste good together. And the combination of sweet and juicy strawberries and tart rhubarb is not an exception. Rhubarb, in fact, is known as a harbinger of spring and all of its tempting offerings. So be tempted and enjoy this delicious fruit and custard pie.

**LET'S BEGIN** Preheat the oven to 425°F. Combine the sugar and flour in a medium bowl. Gently stir in the rhubarb and strawberries until blended. Spoon the rhubarb mixture into the pie shell. Whisk the eggs, milk, and almond extract in the same bowl until well blended. Pour over the rhubarb mixture.

**INTO THE OVEN** Bake for 15 minutes. Reduce the oven temperature to 350°F and bake 25 to 30 minutes longer, until a small knife inserted near the center of the pie comes out clean. Transfer to a wire rack to cool completely. Garnish with strawberries, if you wish.

*Makes 6 servings*

*Per serving: 316 calories, 6g protein, 50g carbohydrates, 10g fat, 2g saturated fat, 107mg cholesterol, 175mg sodium*

# Fresh Peach & Blueberry Pie

*Prep* **25 minutes**   *Bake* **50 minutes**

*Peaches and blueberries are a great flavor combination. For the best taste, plan ahead so your peaches have enough time to ripen.*

| | |
|---|---|
| 1 | (9-inch) unbaked pie shell |
| ½ | cup sugar |
| ¼ | cup all-purpose flour |
| 1 | teaspoon ground cinnamon + extra for topping (optional) |
| 1 | teaspoon vanilla extract |
| 2 | pounds ripe peaches, peeled and thickly sliced (4 cups) |
| 1 | cup fresh blueberries |

## CRUMB TOPPING

| | |
|---|---|
| ¾ | cup all-purpose flour |
| ⅔ | cup sugar |
| ¼ | teaspoon ground nutmeg |
| 6 | tablespoons cold butter, cut up |

Vanilla ice cream (optional)

**LET'S BEGIN** Preheat the oven to 375°F. Prepare the pie shell (do not bake). Combine the sugar, flour, cinnamon, and vanilla in a large bowl. Gently stir in the peaches and blueberries until blended. Spoon the filling into the pie shell. To make the topping, combine the flour, sugar, and nutmeg in a medium bowl. Cut in the butter with a pastry cutter until the mixture resembles coarse crumbs. Sprinkle over filling.

**INTO THE OVEN** Bake the pie on a baking sheet for 50 to 55 minutes, until bubbly in the center. Serve warm or at room temperature. Serve with ice cream sprinkled with a dash of cinnamon, if you wish.

*Makes 8 servings*

*Per serving: 420 calories, 4g protein, 64g carbohydrates, 17g fat, 7g saturated fat, 24mg cholesterol, 182mg sodium*

---

## On the Menu

It's summertime—time for backyard barbecues! Stage a traditional outdoor feast, invite the neighbors, and fire up the grill. End the evening with a classic fresh fruit pie—à la mode, of course.

Minted Lemonade

Creamy Coleslaw

Roasted Potato Salad with Dill

BBQ Ribs

Warm Biscuits

Fresh Peach & Blueberry Pie

Vanilla Ice Cream

# Fresh Blueberry Pie

*Prep* **25 minutes**   *Bake* **50 minutes + cooling**

Pastry for a double-crust 9-inch pie (homemade or store-bought)
1   cup sugar + extra for topping
⅓   cup all-purpose flour
1   tablespoon lemon juice
½   teaspoon grated lemon zest (optional)
4   cups fresh blueberries
2   tablespoons butter or margarine, cut up
Milk

*When it's spring and you see the first blueberries in the market, bake this pie . . . you'll be glad you did!*

**LET'S BEGIN** Preheat the oven to 375°F. On a lightly floured surface, roll half the pastry dough into a ⅛-inch-thick round. Fold in half and ease gently into a 9-inch pie pan. Unfold the dough, letting the pastry overhang the edge. Trim the pastry to 1 inch from the rim of the pan. Set aside.

**FILL IT** Combine the 1 cup sugar, flour, lemon juice, and lemon zest, if desired, in a large bowl. Add the blueberries and toss gently to coat. Spoon into the pie shell and dot with butter. Roll the remaining pastry into a ⅛-inch-thick round and place on top of the filling. Trim and flute the edges. Cut slits in the top crust, brush with milk, and sprinkle with sugar.

**INTO THE OVEN** Bake for 50 minutes until the top is golden brown and the filling is bubbly. Cool 45 minutes on a wire rack. Serve warm or at room temperature.

*Makes 8 servings*

*Per serving: 410 calories, 4g protein, 60g carbohydrates, 18g fat, 5g saturated fat, 8mg cholesterol, 257mg sodium*

## Baking Basics

### THE EASY WAY TO WEAVE A LATTICE TOP

Mix pastry dough for a double-crust pie. Roll out half of the dough. Transfer to a pie plate, shape it, flute it, and fill it. Roll out the remaining dough ⅛ inch thick into a rectangle about 6 × 12 inches. Cut out 12-inch strips crosswise, each ½ inch wide.

Place 1 strip over the center of the pie. Cover it with another long strip. Continue laying strips in the same direction, folding back the center strip every other time.

Now fold back every other strip and lay the cross strips in place. Unfold all the folded-back strips.

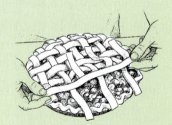

Lastly, trim off the overhangs with kitchen scissors. Seal the edges of the pastry with water to the fluted edge by pinching them.

# DRIED CHERRY APPLE PIE

*Prep* **30 MINUTES**    *Bake* **40 MINUTES**

Pastry dough for a double-crust 9-inch pie

- 4 cups peeled, cored, and sliced apples
- 1 cup dried tart cherries
- 1 cup sugar
- ¼ cup all-purpose flour
- ½ teaspoon ground cinnamon
- 1 tablespoon butter or margarine, cut into pieces

*Dried tart cherries are full of great flavor and they're good for you, too. Buy extra and add some to your next batch of oatmeal cookies or bran muffins.*

**LET'S BEGIN** Preheat the oven to 425°F. On a lightly floured surface, roll half the pastry dough into a ⅛-inch-thick round. Fold in half and ease gently into a 9-inch pie pan. Unfold the dough, letting the pastry overhang the edge. Trim the pastry to 1 inch from the rim of the pan. Refrigerate while making the filling.

**FILLING** Combine the apple slices and cherries in a large bowl. Combine the sugar, flour, and cinnamon in a small bowl. Pour the sugar mixture over the fruit; toss to blend. Let the filling stand at room temperature for 15 minutes. Spoon the filling into the pie shell and dot with the butter. Roll the remaining pastry into a ⅛-inch-thick round and cut into ½-inch strips. Use to weave a lattice top for the pie (see opposite page). Trim and flute the edges.

**INTO THE OVEN** Bake 40 to 50 minutes, until the edge and top of the crust are golden brown and the apples are tender.

*Makes 8 servings*

*Per serving: 460 calories, 4g protein, 78g carbohydrates, 17g fat, 5g saturated fat, 4mg cholesterol, 256mg sodium*

## SuperQuick
# Citrus Mini Tarts

*Prep* **20 minutes**   *Bake* **10 minutes**

- ½ cup freshly squeezed orange juice
- 2 tablespoons firmly packed brown sugar
- 4 (3-inch) prepared puff pastry rounds
- 8 fresh orange segments
- 4 fresh pummelo or grapefruit segments

**ORANGE WHIPPED CREAM**

- ½ cup heavy cream
- 2 tablespoons freshly squeezed orange juice
- 1 tablespoon grated orange zest
- 1 tablespoon confectioners' sugar

*Pummelo, pomelo, and pommelo are all the same citrus fruit, just with different spellings. They are native to Malaysia and are thought to be the ancestor to the grapefruit. Choose a pummelo that is heavy for its size, blemish-free, nice-looking, and fragrant—or use grapefruit.*

**LET'S BEGIN** Stir the orange juice and brown sugar in a small saucepan until the sugar dissolves. Bring to a boil and continue boiling until the mixture is reduced by half to a syrupy consistency. Remove from the heat and cool to room temperature.

**ASSEMBLE & BAKE** Preheat the oven to 425°F. Arrange the puff pastry rounds on a large ungreased cookie sheet. Brush 1 tablespoon of the syrup mixture on each pastry round. Arrange 2 orange segments and 1 pummelo segment on top of each pastry. Bake for 10 to 15 minutes, until puffed and lightly golden brown. Transfer the tarts to wire racks.

**BEAT IT** Meanwhile, to make the orange whipped cream, beat the cream in a small bowl with an electric mixer on medium-high speed until soft peaks form. Beat in all of the remaining ingredients. Continue to beat until stiff. Serve the tarts warm or at room temperature with the orange whipped cream.

*Makes 4 tarts*

*Per tart: 460 calories, 5g protein, 46g carbohydrates, 29g fat, 11g saturated fat, 41mg cholesterol, 132mg sodium*

# Almond & Mixed Berry Tart

*Prep* **30 minutes**   *Bake* **30 minutes + chilling**

## CRUST

- 1½ cups all-purpose flour
- ⅓ cup whole blanched almonds, toasted
- ¼ teaspoon salt
- ½ cup unsalted butter, softened
- ⅓ cup confectioners' sugar
- 1 large egg

## FILLING

- 3 tablespoons almond paste
- 4 tablespoons granulated sugar
- ¼ cup unsalted butter, softened
- 1 large egg
- 3 tablespoons all-purpose flour
- 4 cups assorted fresh berries

*The combination of fresh berries and almonds is a match made in heaven. Here you get double the pleasure, as there are toasted almonds in the crust and flavorful almond paste in the filling. Use a mix of your favorite berries for the uncooked topping.*

**LET'S BEGIN** To make the crust, process the flour, almonds, and salt in a food processor until the almonds are ground. Beat the butter and confectioners' sugar in a large bowl with an electric mixer on medium-high speed until light and fluffy. Beat in the egg. Reduce the speed to low, add the flour mixture, and beat just until blended. Shape the pastry into a thick disk. Wrap in plastic wrap and refrigerate for at least 1 hour until firm.

**ROLL & CHILL** On a lightly floured surface, roll the pastry into a 12-inch circle. Fold pastry in half and ease into a 9-inch round tart pan with a removable bottom. Unfold the pastry and gently press along the bottom and up the sides of the pan. Trim any excess pastry. Prick the crust all over with tines of a fork. Refrigerate for at least 2 hours or cover and refrigerate overnight.

**FILL & BAKE** Preheat the oven to 350°F. To make the filling, beat the almond paste and granulated sugar in a small bowl with an electric mixer at medium speed until no clumps of almond paste remain (mixture should be mealy). Beat in the butter until almost smooth. Add the egg and beat until smooth. Beat in the flour just until blended. Spread the filling evenly in the crust. Bake for 30 minutes, or until the filling is puffy and golden. Cool completely in the pan on a wire rack. Remove the side of the pan and top with the berries.

*Makes 8 servings*

*Per serving: 410 calories, 7g protein, 42g carbohydrates, 25g fat, 12g saturated fat, 101mg cholesterol, 96mg sodium*

# Blue Ribbon Apple Pie

Prep **1 hour**   Bake **45 minutes**

## CRUST

- 2 cups all-purpose flour
- 1 teaspoon granulated sugar
- ¼ teaspoon each salt, ground cinnamon, and ground nutmeg
- ⅓ cup cold butter
- ⅓ cup vegetable shortening
- 4 to 5 tablespoons cold water

## FILLING

- ½ cup + 1 teaspoon granulated sugar
- ¼ cup firmly packed brown sugar
- ¼ cup all-purpose flour
- ½ teaspoon ground cinnamon
- ½ teaspoon ground nutmeg
- 6 medium tart cooking apples, peeled and sliced ¼-inch-thick (6 cups)
- 1 tablespoon butter, melted

*For a perfectly nice and big apple pie, use 6 cups of sliced apples. Choose Granny Smith, Northern Spy, or Rhode Island Greening.*

**LET'S BEGIN** Preheat the oven to 400°F. To make the crust, combine the flour, granulated sugar, salt, cinnamon, and nutmeg in a large bowl. Cut in the butter and shortening with a pastry cutter until the mixture resembles coarse crumbs. Stir in enough of the water with a fork just until the flour mixture is moistened. Divide the dough in half and shape each half into a thick disk. Wrap 1 piece of dough in plastic wrap and refrigerate. On a lightly floured surface, roll out the remaining dough into a 12-inch circle. Transfer into a 9-inch pie pan and press firmly against the bottom and sides. Trim the crust to ½ inch from the edge of the pan and set aside.

**FILL IT** To make the filling, combine ½ cup of the granulated sugar, the brown sugar, flour, cinnamon, and nutmeg in a large bowl. Add the apples and toss gently to coat. Spoon the filling into the prepared crust. Roll the remaining dough into a 12-inch circle and place on top of the pie. Trim and flute the edges. Cut slits in the top crust to allow steam to escape. Brush the top with the melted butter and sprinkle with the remaining 1 teaspoon granulated sugar. Cover the edge of the crust with a 2-inch strip of foil.

**INTO THE OVEN** Bake for 35 minutes and remove the foil. Bake 10 to 20 minutes longer, until the crust is lightly browned and the filling is bubbly. Cool on a wire rack for 30 minutes. Serve warm.

*Makes 8 servings*

Per serving (without cream): 400 calories, 4g protein, 60g carbohydrates, 18g total fat, 7g saturated fat, 25mg cholesterol, 170mg sodium

# Famous Pumpkin Pie

*Prep* **15 minutes**   *Bake* **55 minutes**

- 1 (9-inch) unbaked deep-dish pie shell
- ¾ cup sugar
- 1 teaspoon ground cinnamon
- ½ teaspoon salt
- ½ teaspoon ground ginger
- ¼ teaspoon ground cloves
- 2 large eggs
- 1 can (15 ounces) solid-pack pumpkin
- 1 can (12 ounces) evaporated milk
- Whipped cream (optional)

Could Thanksgiving possibly exist without a custardy pumpkin pie? Probably not. Here is the classic—possibly the best in the world.

**LET'S BEGIN** Preheat the oven to 425°F. Prepare the pie shell in a 9-inch deep-dish pie plate (do not bake).

**MIX IT UP** Combine the sugar, cinnamon, salt, ginger, and cloves in a small bowl. Beat the eggs in a large bowl, then stir in the pumpkin and the sugar-spice mixture. Gradually stir in the evaporated milk. Pour the filling into the pie shell.

**INTO THE OVEN** Bake for 15 minutes. Reduce the oven temperature to 350°F. Bake 40 to 50 minutes longer, until a knife inserted near the center comes out clean. Cool on a wire rack for 2 hours. Serve immediately or refrigerate. Top with whipped cream before serving, if you wish. (Do not freeze this pie, as the crust will separate from the filling.)

*Makes 8 servings*

Per serving: 280 calories, 6g protein, 37g carbohydrates, 12g fat, 4g saturated fat, 65mg cholesterol, 328mg sodium

# Cranberry Pecan Pie

*Prep* **30 MINUTES**   *Bake* **20 MINUTES**

- 1   9-inch fully baked pie shell
- 2   cups fresh or frozen cranberries
- 1   cup orange juice
- ½   cup honey
- 2   tablespoons cornstarch
- 2   tablespoons cold water
- ½   teaspoon orange extract

**HONEY-PECAN TOPPING**

- ½   cup honey
- 3   tablespoons butter or margarine, cut into pieces
- 1¾   cups pecan halves

*Serve with scoops of orange sherbet or vanilla ice cream—or both!*

**LET'S BEGIN** Prepare and bake the pie shell. Adjust the oven temperature to 350°F. Combine the cranberries, orange juice, and honey in a medium saucepan. Cook, uncovered, over low heat for 15 minutes (for fresh) or 20 minutes (for frozen). Cool.

**COOK & FILL** Purée the mixture in a blender and return to the saucepan. Combine the cornstarch and water in a small bowl. Stir into the cranberry mixture. Bring to a boil and cook 1 minute, or until thickened. Stir in the orange extract. Cool, then pour into the pie shell.

**TOP & BAKE** To make the topping, combine the honey and butter in a small saucepan. Cook, stirring, over medium heat until smooth. Stir in the pecans and spoon over the filling. Bake for 20 minutes, or until the filling is bubbly. Serve at room temperature or chilled.

*Makes 8 servings*

*Per serving: 525 calories, 4g protein, 57g carbohydrates, 34g fat, 8g saturated fat, 24mg cholesterol, 190mg sodium*

## Baking Basics

### 3 SIMPLE WAYS TO MAKE A FANCY CRUST

Fluted piecrusts are pretty—and so easy.

**Fluted Edge** Place a thumb against the inside edge of the crust. Then with the thumb and index finger of your other hand about ½ inch apart, press the dough around the thumb to create a fluted shape. Repeat in ½-inch intervals all around.

**Rickrack Flute** Create a fluted edge as directed, then gently squeeze each flute to create a sharp V-shape.

**Rope Edge** Grip the dough firmly between your thumb and index finger at a 45-degree angle and slightly twist the dough outward. Repeat all around at 1-inch intervals.

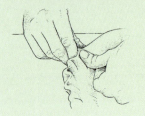
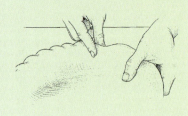

# Rustic Cranberry Apple Tart

*Prep* **15 minutes**    *Bake* **55 minutes**

- 1 refrigerated piecrust (from a 15-ounce package), softened as directed
- 1 can (21 ounces) apple pie filling
- 1 cup fresh or frozen cranberries, chopped
- ¼ cup chopped walnuts (optional)
- 1 teaspoon ground cinnamon
- 1 teaspoon sugar

*The combination of apple, walnuts, and cranberries is the very essence of all of the good flavors that the fall season brings. Here apple pie filling and refrigerated piecrust make this dessert both easy and great tasting. Save even more time—buy pre-chopped walnuts.*

**LET'S BEGIN** Preheat the oven to 400°F. Line the piecrust in a 9-inch pie pan as directed on the package for a one-crust filled pie.

**FILL IT UP** Combine the pie filling, cranberries, walnuts, if desired, and cinnamon in a medium bowl and mix well. Spoon the fruit mixture into the pie shell. Fold the edges of the crust over the filling, pleating them so the crust lies flat and leaving some filling showing in center. Sprinkle the sugar over the crust.

**INTO THE OVEN** Bake for 15 minutes. Reduce the oven temperature to 350°F and bake 40 to 45 minutes longer, until the filling is bubbly and the crust is golden brown. Transfer to a wire rack. Serve warm or at room temperature.

*Makes 8 servings*

*Per serving: 204 calories, 1g protein, 35g carbohydrates, 7g fat, 3g saturated fat, 5mg cholesterol, 133mg sodium*

# LEMON RIBBON ICE CREAM PIE

*Prep* **35 MINUTES + CHILLING + FREEZING**

### CRUST

- 1¼ cups finely crushed pretzels
- ¼ cup granulated sugar
- ½ cup butter or margarine, melted

### FILLING

- 1 cup granulated sugar
- ⅓ cup butter or margarine, melted
- ⅓ cup lemon juice
- 2 teaspoons grated lemon zest
- 4 large eggs, lightly beaten
- ¼ teaspoon salt
- 2 pints vanilla ice cream, slightly softened and divided

### GARNISH

- ¾ cup cold heavy cream
- 1 tablespoon confectioners' sugar
- ½ cup fresh blueberries

*Nothing says refreshing more than lemon and vanilla. This dessert may take a few extra minutes, but the end result is worth every moment. Crushed pretzels make the fabulously crunchy and creative crust. The easy lemon curd filling is so delicious that you might want to cook a double batch so you have some for spooning over breakfast toast, muffins, or fresh blueberries.*

**LET'S BEGIN** To make the crust, mix all of the ingredients together in a medium bowl. Press the mixture evenly in the bottom and up the sides of a 9-inch pie pan. Refrigerate.

**FILL & CHILL** To make the filling, combine the first 6 ingredients in a medium saucepan and mix well. Cook over medium heat, stirring constantly, for 5 to 7 minutes, until the mixture thickens. Transfer the hot lemon filling to a bowl. Cover the surface with plastic wrap or waxed paper. Refrigerate 1 to 2 hours, until thoroughly chilled. Quickly spread 1 pint of the ice cream into the crust. Spoon two-thirds of the chilled lemon filling (about 1½ cups) over the ice cream layer and spread evenly. Freeze for 15 minutes. Spoon the remaining pint of ice cream over the lemon layer, mounding slightly. Freeze for 10 minutes. Spread the remaining lemon filling over the pie. Freeze for 3 to 4 hours until firm.

**GARNISH & SERVE** Let the pie stand at room temperature for 10 minutes before serving. Meanwhile, to make the garnish, beat the cream and confectioners' sugar in a small bowl with an electric mixer until soft peaks form. Cut the pie into wedges and garnish with the whipped cream and blueberries.

*Makes 8 servings*

*Per serving: 720 calories, 9g protein, 63g carbohydrates, 48g fat, 20g saturated fat, 255mg cholesterol, 550mg sodium*

# Frozen Key Lime Torte

*Prep* **20 minutes + freezing**

- 1¼ cups graham cracker crumbs
- 2 tablespoons sugar
- ¼ cup butter or margarine, melted
- 1 pint lime sherbet, softened
- 1 pint lemon sorbet, softened
- 1 pint vanilla frozen yogurt, softened
- 1 tablespoon key lime juice
- ¼ cup flaked sweetened coconut, toasted

*A torte is a type of flourless cake. Here refreshing lime sherbet, lemon sorbet, together with vanilla yogurt and flaked coconut make this torte a tropical treat. Let the sherbet, sorbet, and frozen yogurt set in the refrigerator for about 10 minutes, or just until slightly softened.*

**LET'S BEGIN** Coat the bottom of a 9-inch springform pan with nonstick cooking spray. Combine graham cracker crumbs, sugar, and butter in a small bowl and mix well. Press the crumb mixture into the bottom of the pan. Freeze for 15 minutes, or until firm.

**FILL & FREEZE** Spoon the sherbet, sorbet, and frozen yogurt into a large bowl. Add the lime juice and stir gently until blended. Spoon the filling over the crust, spreading evenly. Sprinkle the top with the coconut and press lightly to adhere. Freeze the torte for 4 hours, or until firm.

**TO SERVE** Run a sharp knife around the edge of the torte to loosen and remove the springform side of the pan. Let the torte stand at room temperature for 10 minutes before serving.

*Makes 10 servings*

*Per serving: 290 calories, 5g protein, 48g carbohydrates, 9g fat, 3g saturated fat, 25mg cholesterol, 170mg sodium*

# Pumpkin Spice Cake

*Prep* **30 minutes**    *Bake* **32 minutes**

Vanilla pudding and pie filling mix make this cake especially moist. If you don't want to cook up fresh pumpkin, use canned solid-pack pumpkin (not pumpkin pie mix) instead.

## CAKE

- 1 package (18.25 ounces) yellow cake mix
- 1 package (3-ounce size) vanilla instant pudding and pie filling mix
- 1 cup mashed cooked fresh pumpkin
- ½ cup vegetable oil
- ½ cup water
- 3 large eggs
- 1 tablespoon pumpkin pie spice

## CREAM CHEESE FROSTING

- 1 package (8 ounces) cream cheese, softened
- ¼ cup butter or margarine, softened
- 1 teaspoon vanilla extract
- 1 package (16 ounces) confectioners' sugar, sifted
- ½ cup chopped toasted pecans

**LET'S BEGIN** Preheat the oven to 350°F. Grease and flour a 13 × 9-inch baking pan.

**MIX IT UP** Beat all of the ingredients for the cake in a large bowl with an electric mixer on low speed just until moistened. Increase the speed to medium and beat for 4 minutes. Pour the batter into the pan.

**BAKE & FROST** Bake for 32 to 35 minutes, until a wooden toothpick inserted in the center comes out clean. Transfer the cake to a wire rack and cool completely in the pan. To make the cream cheese frosting, beat the cream cheese, butter, and vanilla in a large bowl with an electric mixer on medium speed until well blended. Gradually add the confectioners' sugar, beating until well blended after each addition. Spread on the top of the cake and sprinkle with the pecans.

### Makes 24 servings

*Per serving: 290 calories, 2g protein, 41g carbohydrates, 14g fat, 5g saturated fat, 42mg cholesterol, 220mg sodium*

# CRANBERRY PUMPKIN CHEESECAKE

*Prep* **15 MINUTES**  *Bake* **1 HOUR + STANDING + CHILLING**

- 2 cups gingersnap cookie crumbs
- ¼ cup butter or margarine, melted
- 3 packages (8 ounces each) cream cheese, softened
- ⅓ cup firmly packed brown sugar
- ⅓ cup confectioners' sugar
- 2 tablespoons all-purpose flour
- 1 tablespoon pumpkin pie spice
- 2 large eggs
- 1 can (15 ounces) solid-pack pumpkin
- 1 can (16 ounces) whole berry cranberry sauce

*Here's a dessert that's destined to be the centerpiece at your next Thanksgiving celebration. The cheesecake is best baked at least one day ahead, so there is no last-minute baking to worry about. For the neatest slices, use a thin knife dipped in hot water between each cut.*

**LET'S BEGIN** Preheat the oven to 350°F. Combine the gingersnap crumbs and butter in a medium bowl until the crumbs are evenly moistened. Press the crumb mixture evenly over the bottom and 2 inches up the sides of a 10-inch springform pan.

**MIX IT UP** Beat the cream cheese, brown sugar, confectioners' sugar, flour, and pie spice in a large bowl with an electric mixer until smooth. Beat in the eggs and pumpkin until well blended. Pour the filling into the pan.

**INTO THE OVEN** Place the cheesecake on a large cookie sheet and bake for 1 hour. Turn off the oven and let the cheesecake stand in the oven for 1 hour more. (Do not open the oven door.) Transfer the cheesecake to a wire rack and cool completely. Cover and refrigerate at least 6 hours or overnight. To serve, run a sharp knife around the edge to loosen the cheesecake and remove the springform side of the pan. Top with cranberry sauce.

*Makes 12 servings*

*Per serving: 429 calories, 7g protein, 43g carbohydrates, 26g fat, 15g saturated fat, 108mg cholesterol, 352mg sodium*

# Holiday Eggnog Cake

*Prep* **15 minutes**   *Bake* **50 minutes + standing**

## CAKE

- 1 package (18.25 ounces) yellow cake mix
- 1 cup prepared eggnog
- ⅓ cup water
- ¼ cup butter, melted and cooled slightly
- 3 large eggs
- ½ teaspoon ground nutmeg

## GLAZE

- 1 cup confectioners' sugar
- 2 tablespoons hot melted butter
- 1½ tablespoons hot milk

Ground nutmeg (optional)

Sweetened whipped cream (optional)

*Nothing says holiday better than eggnog—except perhaps eggnog-infused cake. Prepared eggnog is readily available during the winter in the dairy aisle of supermarkets. It's tasty and no work—a perfect combination.*

**LET'S BEGIN** Preheat the oven to 350°F. Grease and flour a 12-cup Bundt cake pan. Beat all of the ingredients for the cake in a large bowl with an electric mixer on medium speed for 2 minutes, until well mixed. Pour the batter into the pan.

**INTO THE OVEN** Bake for 50 minutes, or until the cake is golden brown and comes slightly away from the edge of the pan. Cool in the pan for 10 minutes. Turn upside down onto a wire rack and remove the pan. Cool completely.

**GLAZE IT** To make the glaze, whisk the confectioners' sugar, butter, and milk in a medium bowl until smooth. Place the cake on a serving plate. Spoon the warm glaze over the cake, letting the excess drip down the sides. Sprinkle the glaze with nutmeg, if you wish. Let the cake stand for 10 minutes, or until the glaze is set. Serve with whipped cream, if desired.

**Makes 12 servings**

*Per serving: 328 calories, 4g protein, 47g carbohydrates, 14g fat, 5g saturated fat, 83mg cholesterol, 356mg sodium*

# Holiday Fruited Pound Cake

Prep **25 minutes**    Bake **1 hour**

- 1½ cups sugar
- 1 cup butter, softened
- 4 ounces cream cheese, softened
- 6 large eggs
- 1 tablespoon grated orange zest
- 1 tablespoon vanilla extract
- 1 teaspoon brandy extract
- 1 teaspoon rum extract
- 3 cups all-purpose flour
- ½ teaspoon baking powder
- ½ cup green candied cherries, coarsely chopped + extra for garnish (optional)
- ½ cup red candied cherries, coarsely chopped + extra for garnish (optional)
- ½ cup raisins
- Rum Glaze (see recipe)

*Fruit cake studded with green and red candied cherries is enough to put anyone in a festive holiday mood. A blend of butter and cream cheese makes this pound cake especially moist and tender.*

**LET'S BEGIN** Preheat the oven to 350°F. Grease and flour a 12-cup Bundt cake pan or 10-inch tube pan.

**MIX IT UP** To make the cake, beat the sugar, butter, and cream cheese in a large bowl with an electric mixer on medium speed, scraping the bowl often, until light and fluffy. Add the eggs, one at a time, beating well after each addition and scraping the bowl often. Beat in the orange zest and the vanilla, brandy, and rum extracts. Reduce the speed to low and beat in the flour and baking powder just until blended. Stir in the candied cherries and raisins by hand. Spoon the batter into the pan.

**INTO THE OVEN** Bake for 60 to 70 minutes, until a wooden toothpick inserted in the center comes out clean. Cool in the pan for 10 minutes. Turn upside down onto a wire rack and remove the pan. Cool completely. Meanwhile, make the Rum Glaze. Drizzle it over the top, letting it run down the side. Garnish the cake with the candied cherries, if you wish.

## Rum Glaze

Combine in a small bowl: ¾ cup confectioners' sugar, ½ teaspoon rum extract, and 1 tablespoon milk, adding more milk if necessary to reach glazing consistency.

### Makes 16 servings

Per serving: 400 calories, 6g protein, 57g carbohydrates, 16g total fat, 8g saturated fat, 120mg cholesterol, 190mg sodium

Merry Meringue Cake, page 121

# Celebrations!

It's time to celebrate! Whether it's someone's birthday, your favorite holiday, or just a romantic dinner for two, why not bake a fancy cake or a delicious pie? You'll find many perfect recipes by just turning the page. Start with the traditional: a lush yellow cake with a rich buttercream that's exactly the kind that has won blue ribbons for generations. Go for the fresh lemon pie with a perfect meringue that would win even the stiffest competition. When it's Easter, celebrate by turning an easy cake into a fancy bonnet that's showered with coconut and flowers. Toast the Fourth of July with a cake that looks like a flag. Or whip up a special cheesecake anytime to create unforgettable memories.

# BIRTHDAY CAKE

*Prep* **25 MINUTES**    *Bake* **28 MINUTES + COOLING**

## CAKE

- 3 cups all-purpose flour
- 1 tablespoon baking powder
- ½ teaspoon salt
- 1½ cups granulated sugar
- ¾ cup butter, softened
- 4 large eggs
- 1 tablespoon vanilla extract
- 1 cup milk

## BIRTHDAY FROSTING

- ¾ cup butter, softened
- 6 cups confectioners' sugar
- ⅛ teaspoon salt
- ⅓ cup cold heavy cream
- 1 teaspoon vanilla extract
- 2 tablespoons light corn syrup

*Sometimes simple is best. This plain—but rich—butter cake has lots of enticing vanilla flavoring in both the cake and the frosting. The amount of extract called for may seem like a lot, but it's actually just perfect.*

**LET'S BEGIN** Preheat the oven to 350°F. Grease and flour two 9-inch round cake pans. To make the cake, combine the flour, baking powder, and salt in a large bowl. Beat the sugar and butter in a large bowl with an electric mixer on medium speed, scraping the bowl occasionally, until light and fluffy. Add the eggs, one at a time, beating well after each addition. Add the vanilla. Reduce the speed to low. Add the flour mixture, alternately with the milk, beginning and ending with the flour mixture and beating well after each addition. Divide the batter evenly between the pans.

**INTO THE OVEN** Bake for 28 to 33 minutes, until a wooden toothpick inserted in the center comes out clean. Cool in the pans for 10 minutes. Loosen the cakes by running a knife around the inside edge of the pans. Carefully remove the cakes from the pans and cool completely on wire racks.

**FROST & ASSEMBLE** To make the frosting, beat the butter in a large bowl with an electric mixer on medium speed until creamy. Gradually add the confectioners' sugar and salt alternately with the cream and vanilla, scraping the bowl often, until well mixed. Stir in the corn syrup. To assemble, place one cake layer on a serving plate, bottom side up, and frost the top. Place remaining cake layer over the frosting, bottom side down, and frost the top and sides of the cake.

*Makes 12 servings*

*Per serving: 680 calories, 6g protein, 103g carbohydrates, 28g total fat, 14g saturated fat, 120mg cholesterol, 450mg sodium*

## Cooking Basics

### 3 EASY STEPS FOR ICING A LAYER CAKE

Some recipes call for splitting the cake layers in half. Be sure the layers are completely cooled or else they will fall apart when cut.

First make a shallow vertical cut, so you can line up the layers later. Using a long serrated knife and a gentle sawing motion, cut each layer horizontally in half. You can also mark the middle of each layer by inserting toothpicks all around, then cut just above the toothpicks.

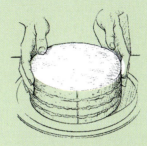

Place one cake layer on a cake plate and spread with the directed amount of frosting. Top with another layer, lining up the vertical cuts. Repeat frosting and stacking with the remaining layers. Brush off any loose crumbs using a soft pastry brush.

Using a narrow metal spatula, spread a very thin layer of frosting over the top and sides of the cake to seal in any stray crumbs. Then cover the top and sides of the cake with the remaining frosting, being sure to spread it all the way to the edge. Finish off by either smoothing the frosting or swirling the frosting in fancy peaks.

CELEBRATIONS! 105

# Cherry-Chocolate Heart

*Prep* **30 minutes**   *Bake* **18 minutes + cooling**

- 1 package (15 ounces) refrigerated piecrusts
- 2 teaspoons all-purpose flour
- 1 package (8 ounces) cream cheese, softened
- 1 cup confectioners' sugar
- 1 teaspoon almond extract
- ½ cup heavy cream
- ⅔ cup hot fudge ice cream topping
- 1 can (21 ounces) cherry pie filling and topping

*Be sure to leave enough time for the cream cheese to come to room temperature. It usually takes about 30 minutes.*

**LET'S BEGIN** Preheat the oven to 450°F. Allow both crusts to stand at room temperature for 15 to 20 minutes. Meanwhile, to make a heart-shaped pattern, cut a piece of paper into a heart shape about 10½ inches high and 10 inches wide and set aside. Unfold one of the crusts. Press out the fold lines. (If the crust cracks, wet your fingers and push the edges together.) Sprinkle 1 teaspoon of the flour over the crust. Invert the crust, floured side down, onto a large ungreased cookie sheet. Using the pattern as a guide, cut the crust into a heart shape. Generously prick the heart-shaped crust with a fork. Bake for 9 to 11 minutes, or until lightly browned. Transfer the crust to a wire rack and cool completely. Repeat the process with the remaining crust and 1 teaspoon flour.

**BEAT IT** Combine the cream cheese, confectioners' sugar, and almond extract in a medium bowl with an electric mixer until smooth. Add the cream and beat until thickened.

**ASSEMBLE** Place 1 heart-shaped piecrust on a serving plate and spread ⅓ cup of the fudge over the crust. Carefully spread half the cream cheese mixture over the fudge. Spoon two-thirds of the cherry filling over the cream cheese. Spread the remaining crust with the remaining fudge and place on top of the tart. Carefully spread the remaining cream cheese mixture over the fudge. Spoon the remaining cherry filling on the top, leaving a 1-inch border. Refrigerate until ready to serve.

**Makes 8 servings**

*Per serving: 620 calories, 5g protein, 77g carbohydrates, 32g fat, 17g saturated fat, 63mg cholesterol, 420mg sodium*

# Easter Bonnet Cake

*Prep* **15 minutes + decorating**  *Bake* **40 minutes + cooling**

- 15 Chocolate sandwich cookies
- 1 package (18.25 ounces) yellow cake mix with pudding
- 3 large eggs
- ¼ cup vegetable oil
- 1¼ cups water
- 1 tub (16 ounces) prepared vanilla frosting
- 1⅓ cups sweetened flaked coconut
- Candies for decorating cupcakes (optional)

*Celebrate Easter with this pretty-as-a-picture cake.*

**LET'S BEGIN** Preheat the oven to 350°F. Grease and flour a 9-inch round cake pan and a 10-ounce ovenproof glass custard cup. Line eight 2- to 3-inch muffin cups with paper liners. Split 11 of the cookies in half, leaving the filling on one side of each cookie. Reserve the split cookies with the filling for the brim of the hat. Coarsely chop the plain split cookies and the remaining 4 whole cookies. Set aside.

**MIX & BAKE** Beat the cake mix, oil, eggs, and water in a large bowl with an electric mixer on low speed until moistened. Increase the speed to medium and beat for 2 minutes. Stir in the chopped cookies. Pour 3 cups of the batter into the cake pan and ¾ cup of the batter into the custard cup. Bake for 25 to 30 minutes, until a wooden toothpick inserted in the center of each comes out clean. Divide the remaining batter into the muffin pan cups. Bake for 15 to 25 minutes, until a wooden toothpick inserted in the centers comes out clean. Let the cakes and cupcakes stand in the pans for 10 minutes. Remove from the pans and cool completely on wire racks.

**ASSEMBLE & DECORATE** Reserve ⅓ cup of the frosting for the cupcakes. Arrange the 9-inch cake layer on a serving plate, and frost the top with some of the frosting. Place the round cake from the custard cup, top side down and slightly off-center, on top. Frost the side and top of the "bonnet" with the remaining frosting. Sprinkle the cake with the coconut, pressing gently into the frosting. Cut the reserved 11 split cookies in half, and place, filling side up and rounded edge out, around the brim of the hat. Decorate the cupcakes with the reserved frosting and the candies.

*Makes 16 servings*
*Per serving: 390 calories, 3g protein, 58g carbohydrates, 17g fat, 7g saturated fat, 40mg cholesterol, 380mg sodium*

# Banana Chiffon Cake

*Prep* **20 MINUTES**     *Bake* **1 HOUR 15 MINUTES + COOLING**

- 2¼ cups sifted cake flour (not self-rising)
- 1½ cups superfine sugar
- 1 tablespoon baking powder
- 1 teaspoon salt
- ¼ teaspoon ground nutmeg (optional)
- 1 cup (3 to 4) mashed extra-ripe bananas
- ½ cup vegetable oil
- 5 large egg yolks
- ⅓ cup water
- 1 teaspoon vanilla extract
- 1 cup egg whites, at room temperature (about 12 large egg whites)
- ½ teaspoon cream of tartar

*When making a chiffon or angle food cake, be sure to fold a portion of the stiffly beaten egg whites into the cake batter first. This makes the batter light and airy. Then the rest of the beaten whites can be folded in faster, easier, and with fewer folding strokes. The result? A lighter, higher cake!*

**LET'S BEGIN** Preheat the oven to 300°F. Sift together the flour, 1¼ cups of the sugar, baking powder, salt, and nutmeg, if desired, in a large bowl. Make a well in the center of the flour mixture. Whisk the bananas, oil, egg yolks, water, and vanilla in a medium bowl until smooth. Pour into the center of the flour mixture. Gradually whisk the liquid ingredients into the flour mixture until smooth.

**MIX IT UP** Beat the egg whites and cream of tartar in a large bowl with an electric mixer on medium-high speed until soft peaks form. Add the remaining ¼ cup sugar, 1 tablespoon at a time. Increase the speed to high and beat until the egg whites are stiff but not dry. With a rubber spatula, gently fold one-third of the whites into the banana mixture. Repeat twice more with the remaining whites just until blended. (Do not overmix.) Pour the batter into an ungreased 10-inch tube pan.

**INTO THE OVEN** Bake for 1 hour. Increase the oven temperature to 350°F and bake 15 minutes longer, or until the cake springs back when touched lightly. Immediately invert the pan onto a funnel or bottle. Cool completely. Run a metal spatula or knife around the sides of the pan and the tube. Invert to unmold.

*Makes 12 servings*

Per serving: 318 calories, 7g protein, 48g carbohydrates, 11g fat, 2g saturated fat, 85mg cholesterol, 314mg sodium

# Red, White & Blue Cheesecake

*Prep* **25 minutes**   *Bake* **1 hour + chilling**

## CRUST

| | |
|---|---|
| 1 | cup finely crushed graham crackers |
| ¼ | cup sugar |
| ¼ | cup butter or margarine, melted |

## FILLING

| | |
|---|---|
| 4 | cups (30 ounces) light ricotta cheese |
| ¾ | cup sugar |
| ½ | cup half-and-half |
| ¼ | cup all-purpose flour |
| 1 | teaspoon vanilla extract |
| ¼ | teaspoon salt |
| 3 | large eggs |
| ½ | cup blueberry fruit spread, heated |
| 1½ | cups fresh strawberry slices or fresh whole raspberries |
| ½ | cup fresh blueberries |
| ¼ | cup red currant jelly, heated |

*Ricotta cheesecakes are usually lighter than the more traditional cream cheese cakes. Italians have been enjoying them forever.*

**LET'S BEGIN** To make the crust, combine all of the ingredients in a small bowl until the crumbs are evenly moistened. Press evenly over the bottom and 1½ inches up the sides of an 8- or 9-inch springform pan. Refrigerate while preparing the filling.

**MIX IT UP** To make the filling, preheat the oven to 350°F. Beat the first 6 ingredients in a large bowl with an electric mixer on medium-high speed until smooth. Add the eggs, one at a time, beating well after each addition. Pour half the batter over the crust. Spoon half of the blueberry spread randomly over the batter. Top with the remaining batter and smooth with a spatula. Spoon the remaining blueberry spread randomly over the batter. Swirl a knife through the batter and blueberry spread to marbleize.

**INTO THE OVEN** Bake for 1 hour, or until the center is just set. Turn off the oven and cool the cheesecake in the oven with the door propped open for 30 minutes. Transfer to a wire rack. Loosen the cake from the rim of the pan with a metal spatula. Cool completely.

**CHILL & SERVE** Refrigerate at least 2 hours, or cover and refrigerate up to 24 hours. Remove the springform side of the pan. Arrange the strawberries and blueberries around the edge of the cheesecake. Brush the jelly over the fruit. Refrigerate at least 30 minutes to set the glaze.

**Makes 12 servings**
Per serving: 443 calories, 13g protein, 66g carbohydrates, 15g fat, 8g saturated fat, 128mg cholesterol, 271mg sodium

# Star Spangled Cocoa Bundt

Prep **20 minutes**  Bake **45 minutes + cooling**

- 2 cups all-purpose flour
- ⅔ cup unsweetened cocoa
- ½ teaspoon salt
- ¾ cup butter or margarine, softened
- 1⅔ cups granulated sugar
- 2 large eggs
- 1 teaspoon vanilla extract
- ¾ cup sour cream
- 2 teaspoons baking soda
- 1 cup buttermilk or sour milk (see note)

Confectioners' sugar

Fresh blueberries, strawberries, and sweetened whipped cream (optional)

*Baking soda is vital to recipes that contain cocoa, sour cream, or buttermilk. Store it in a cool, dry place for up to 6 months, then replace it. Open the top of the box of the outdated soda, and pop it into the refrigerator to absorb any odors.*

**LET'S BEGIN** Preheat the oven to 350°F. Grease and flour a 12-cup Bundt cake pan.

**MIX IT UP** Combine the flour, cocoa, and salt in a medium bowl. Beat the butter, granulated sugar, eggs, and vanilla in a large bowl with an electric mixer on medium speed until fluffy. Beat in the sour cream. Stir the baking soda into the buttermilk in a small bowl. Alternately add the flour mixture with the buttermilk mixture, beginning and ending with the flour mixture, just until blended. Beat for 2 minutes. Pour the batter into the pan.

**INTO THE OVEN** Bake for 45 to 50 minutes, until a wooden toothpick inserted in the center comes out clean. Cool in the pan for 10 minutes. Turn upside down onto a wire rack and remove the pan. Cool completely. Place the cake on a serving plate. Sift confectioners' sugar over the top and sides of the cake. Serve with blueberries, strawberries, and whipped cream, if you wish.

**NOTE:** To make sour milk, as a general rule and for this recipe, stir 1 tablespoon white vinegar into 1 cup of milk to turn it sour.

*Makes 12 servings*

Per serving: 350 calories, 5g protein, 48g carbohydrates, 17g fat, 8g saturated fat, 74mg cholesterol, 434mg sodium

# Flag Cookie Cake

*Prep* **15 minutes**   *Bake* **15 minutes + cooling + decorating**

- 1 package (18 ounces) refrigerator sugar cookies
- 1 large egg white, lightly beaten
- 1 package (8 ounces) cream cheese, softened
- ½ cup + 2 tablespoons confectioners' sugar
- ¼ teaspoon almond extract
- 2 cups sliced fresh strawberries or whole raspberries
- 1 cup sliced fresh blackberries or whole blueberries
- Assorted prepared icings, gels, decorator sugars, and cinnamon red hot candies

*This flag cake is easy and unusual. The base is made from refrigerated cookie dough instead of the more usual yellow cake.*

**LET'S BEGIN** Preheat the oven to 375°F. Cut the cookie dough with a sharp knife into ¼-inch-thick slices. Arrange the slices on a 10 × 15-inch jelly-roll pan, pressing the dough evenly to cover the bottom of the pan. Lightly brush the dough with the egg white.

**BAKE & ICE** Bake for 10 minutes, until lightly browned. Cool completely on a wire rack. Beat the cream cheese, ½ cup of the confectioners' sugar, and almond extract in a medium bowl with an electric mixer on medium-high speed until light and fluffy. Spread evenly over the baked cookie crust. Bake for 5 minutes, then cool completely.

**DECORATE** Dust the cookie with the remaining 2 tablespoons confectioners' sugar. Decorate as desired to resemble a flag using the berries, icings, gels, decorator sugars, and candies. If using sliced fruit, drain on paper towels so the colors won't bleed into the icing. Refrigerate until ready to serve.

*Makes 20 servings*
*Per serving: 176 calories, 2g protein, 20g carbohydrates, 10g total fat, 4g saturated fat, 20mg cholesterol, 161mg sodium*

# Chocolate Touchdown Cake

**Prep 30 MINUTES    Bake 35 MINUTES + COOLING + DECORATING**

## CAKE

| | |
|---|---|
| 2 | cups granulated sugar |
| 2¼ | cups all-purpose flour |
| ⅔ | cup unsweetened cocoa |
| 1½ | teaspoons baking soda |
| 1 | teaspoon salt |
| ½ | teaspoon baking powder |
| ¾ | cup water |
| ½ | cup vegetable oil |
| 3 | large eggs |
| 1 | container (8 ounces) sour cream |

Chocolate Buttercream Frosting (see recipe)

## JELLY GLAZE

| | |
|---|---|
| 1 | cup seedless raspberry jam |
| 1 | tablespoon water |

## DECORATOR'S ICING

| | |
|---|---|
| ¾ | cup confectioners' sugar |
| 2 | tablespoons butter or margarine, softened |
| 1 | tablespoon cold water |

*Impress the team with this treat that looks like a football but tastes like the rich, fudgy cake it really is!*

**LET'S BEGIN** Preheat the oven to 350°F. Line a 13 × 9-inch baking pan with foil. Generously grease and flour the foil and set aside. To make the cake, stir the first 6 ingredients in a large bowl with an electric mixer on low speed until mixed well. Beat in the water, oil, and eggs. Increase the speed to medium and beat 2 minutes. Stir in the sour cream and pour into pan.

**INTO THE OVEN** Bake for 35 to 45 minutes, until a wooden toothpick inserted in the center comes out clean. Cool completely on a wire rack. Invert the cake onto a large platter and remove the pan and foil. Trim the top and the edges. Cut in half horizontally into 2 layers.

**FROST & DECORATE** Make the Chocolate Buttercream Frosting and use some to frost the top of 1 cake layer. Top with remaining cake layer and cut into an oval football shape. To make the Glaze, combine the jam and water in a small saucepan. Bring to a boil over medium heat. Cool. Brush the top and sides with the glaze, then let stand 1 hour to dry. Frost the top and sides with the remaining frosting. To make the Icing, beat all of the ingredients with an electric mixer on medium speed for 2 minutes. (Add water to thin if necessary.) Use to fill a pastry bag, fitted with a basket weave tip, and pipe laces on the football cake.

## Chocolate Buttercream Frosting

*In a large bowl, combine one 16-ounce package confectioners' sugar, ½ cup butter or margarine, two 1-ounce squares unsweetened chocolate (melted and cooled), 2 tablespoons milk, and 1 teaspoon vanilla extract. Using an electric mixer, beat on low until blended. Increase the speed to medium and beat 1 to 2 minutes.*

Makes 12 servings

*Per serving: 724 calories, 6g protein, 118g carbohydrates, 28g fat, 11g saturated fat, 88mg cholesterol, 474mg sodium*

# Fresh Lemon Meringue Pie

*Prep* **20 MINUTES**   *Bake* **15 MINUTES + COOLING**

- 1½ cups sugar
- ¼ cup + 2 tablespoons cornstarch
- ¼ teaspoon salt
- ½ cup cold water
- ½ cup lemon juice
- 3 large egg yolks, well beaten
- 2 tablespoons butter or margarine, cut up
- 1½ cups boiling water
- Grated zest of ½ lemon
- 2 drops yellow food coloring (optional)
- 1 9-inch fully baked piecrust

**THREE-EGG MERINGUE**

- 3 large egg whites
- ¼ teaspoon cream of tartar
- 6 tablespoons sugar

*Here is a method for making the prettiest swirls in meringue. First spread the meringue over the filling, creating a dome shape. Make sure that the meringue touches the piecrust all around. Then, using a teaspoon, form dramatic peaks and swirls all over.*

**LET'S BEGIN** Preheat the oven to 350°F. Combine the sugar, cornstarch, and salt in a large saucepan. Gradually whisk in the cold water and lemon juice until smooth. Whisk in the egg yolks, then add the butter and boiling water. Bring the mixture to a boil over medium-high heat, stirring constantly. Reduce the heat to medium and boil for 1 minute. Remove the pan from the heat and stir in the lemon zest and food coloring, if desired. Pour the filling into the piecrust, cover with plastic wrap, and keep hot.

**MAKE TOPPING** To make the meringue, beat the egg whites and cream of tartar in a large bowl with an electric mixer on medium-high speed until foamy. Add the sugar, 1 tablespoon at a time. Increase the speed to high and beat until stiff peaks form. Uncover the filling. Spoon the meringue over the filling, spreading it onto the edge of the piecrust to form a tight seal.

**INTO THE OVEN** Bake for 12 to 15 minutes, until the meringue peaks are golden brown. Cool on a wire rack for 2 hours before serving.

*Makes 8 servings*

*Per serving: 373 calories, 4g protein, 63g carbohydrates, 13g fat, 4g saturated fat, 85mg cholesterol, 242mg sodium*

# Honey Passover Cheesecake

Prep **25 minutes**  Bake **1 hour, 3 minutes + chilling**

**MATZO MEAL TART SHELL**

- 1 cup matzo meal
- 1/3 cup butter, softened
- 1/3 cup water
- 1 tablespoon honey

**FILLING**

- 2 packages (8 ounces each) reduced-fat cream cheese (Neufchâtel), softened
- 2 cups low-fat sour cream
- 2/3 cup honey
- 3 large eggs
- 2 teaspoons vanilla extract

Sliced kiwifruit and strawberries (optional)

*Passover desserts must be flourless and contain no leavening product. This moist honey-flavored cheesecake fits the bill to a tee.*

**LET'S BEGIN** Preheat the oven to 350°F. To make the matzo meal tart shell, process the matzo meal in a food processor until very fine. Add butter and pulse until the mixture resembles coarse meal. Transfer to a bowl. Combine water and honey in a small bowl and mix well. Sprinkle over the matzo mixture. Mix lightly to form a dough and shape into a ball. Press the dough into the bottom of a 9-inch springform pan. Bake for 12 minutes, or until the edges begin to brown. Cool on a wire rack.

**MAKE THE FILLING** To make the filling, beat the cream cheese with 1/2 cup of the sour cream in a large bowl with an electric mixer on low speed until very smooth. Set aside 2 tablespoons of the honey. Increase the speed to medium, gradually beat the remaining honey into the cream cheese mixture. Beat in the eggs, one at a time. Mix in 1 teaspoon of the vanilla and pour into cooled crust.

**BAKE & TOP** Bake for 45 minutes, or until a wooden toothpick inserted near the center comes out clean. Cool for 15 minutes. Meanwhile, increase the oven temperature to 425°F. In a medium bowl, combine the remaining 1 1/2 cups sour cream, the reserved 2 tablespoons honey, and the remaining 1 teaspoon vanilla and mix well. Carefully spread the mixture over the top of cake. Bake for 8 minutes, or until the edges pull away from sides of pan. Transfer to a wire rack and cool completely. Refrigerate until chilled, at least 2 hours, or cover and refrigerate overnight. Run a sharp knife around the edge to loosen the cake and remove the springform side of the pan. Garnish with kiwifruit and strawberries, if you wish.

*Makes 16 servings*

*Per serving: 218 calories, 6g protein, 21g carbohydrates, 14g fat, 8g saturated fat, 83mg cholesterol, 224mg sodium*

# Honey Chiffon Cake

*Prep* **20 minutes**    *Bake* **55 minutes + cooling**

| | |
|---|---|
| 1 | cup all-purpose flour |
| 2 | teaspoons ground cinnamon |
| 1 | teaspoon baking powder |
| ½ | teaspoon baking soda |
| ¼ | teaspoon salt |
| 5 | large eggs, separated |
| ½ | cup sugar |
| ½ | cup honey |
| ½ | cup vegetable oil |
| ½ | teaspoon grated lemon zest (optional) |
| 1 | teaspoon lemon juice |

*Chiffon cake is a foam-type cake. It gets its volume from beaten egg yolks and egg whites and its moistness from vegetable oil. Like angel food cake, it is baked in an ungreased tube pan.*

**LET'S BEGIN** Preheat the oven to 350°F. Combine the flour, cinnamon, baking powder, baking soda, and salt in a medium bowl and mix well.

**MIX IT UP** Beat the egg yolks and sugar in a large bowl with an electric mixer on medium-high speed until thick and lemon-colored. Beat in the honey and oil until blended. Beat in the lemon zest and juice, if you wish. Reduce the mixer speed to low, add the flour mixture into the honey mixture until well blended. Beat the egg whites in another large bowl with an electric mixer until stiff peaks form. With a rubber spatula, gently fold one-third of the whites into the honey mixture. Repeat twice more with the remaining whites just until blended. (Do not overmix.) Pour the batter into an ungreased 9-inch tube pan.

**INTO THE OVEN** Bake for 55 minutes, or until the cake springs back when lightly touched. Immediately invert the pan onto a funnel or bottle. Cool completely. Run a metal spatula or knife around the sides of the pan and tube. Invert to unmold.

*Makes 12 servings*

*Per serving: 223 calories, 4g protein, 28g carbohydrates, 11g fat, 2g saturated fat, 88mg cholesterol, 151mg sodium*

# Pumpkin Faces

*Prep* **20 minutes**  *Bake* **13 minutes + cooling + decorating**

- 1 cup sugar
- ¼ cup + 2 tablespoons unsweetened cocoa
- ½ cup + 2 tablespoons butter-flavor shortening, melted
- 2 large eggs
- ¾ cup all-purpose flour
- 1 teaspoon vanilla extract
- Dash of salt
- ½ cup peanut butter chips
- ½ cup chopped walnuts (optional)
- Frosting for the Pumpkins (see recipe)

*Happy pumpkin faces make these brownie cupcakes the perfect way to celebrate Halloween.*

**LET'S BEGIN** Preheat the oven to 350°F. Place twenty-four 2-inch foil muffin cups on a large cookie sheet. Combine the sugar and cocoa in a large bowl. Add the shortening. Stir with a spoon until well blended. Add the eggs, one at a time, stirring well after each addition. Stir in the flour, vanilla, and salt until well blended. Stir in the peanut butter chips and walnuts, if you wish. Spoon an equal amount of batter into each muffin cup. Bake for 13 to 15 minutes. Cool completely on wire racks.

**FROST & DECORATE** Meanwhile, make the frosting and use it to ice the brownie cups. Place the green and chocolate frostings in separate resealable plastic bags and seal. Snip off one corner of each bag. To decorate, squeeze out the green frosting for the stems and the chocolate frosting for the faces.

## Frosting for the Pumpkins

*Place in a large bowl: one 16-ounce package (4½ cups) confectioners' sugar, ½ cup butter-flavor shortening, ¼ cup milk, 1½ teaspoons vanilla, and ½ teaspoon salt. Using an electric mixer, beat on medium speed for 3 minutes until blended. Increase the speed to high and beat for 5 minutes. (Add more confectioners' sugar to thicken the frosting or more milk to thin it, if necessary.) Remove 1 cup of the frosting and divide it equally between 2 small bowls. Stir 1½ teaspoons cocoa into ½ cup of the frosting until blended. Tint the other ½ cup frosting with a few drops of green food coloring. Add 6 drops yellow food coloring and 4 drops red food coloring to the remaining frosting to tint it orange.*

> **Makes 2 dozen pumpkin faces**
> *Per pumpkin face: 254 calories, 2g protein, 37g carbohydrates, 11g fat, 4g saturated fat, 18mg cholesterol, 77mg sodium*

# Boo the Friendly Ghost Cake

*Prep* **25 minutes**   *Bake* **45 minutes + cooling + decorating**

- 2½ cups all-purpose flour
- 1¼ teaspoons baking soda
- 1 cup firmly packed light brown sugar
- 1 cup granulated sugar
- ⅔ cup butter or margarine, softened
- 3 squares (1 ounce each) unsweetened baking chocolate, melted and cooled
- ½ teaspoon salt
- 2 large eggs
- 1 teaspoon vanilla extract
- 1¼ cups cold water
- Seven Minute Frosting (see recipe)
- Black jelly beans or candies

*Conjure up lots of ghosts and goblins with this Halloween cake.*

**LET'S BEGIN** Preheat the oven to 350°F. Grease and flour a 13 × 9-inch baking pan. Line the pan with waxed or parchment paper. Grease the paper. Combine the flour and baking soda in a small bowl. Beat the brown sugar, granulated sugar, butter, chocolate, and salt in a large bowl with an electric mixer on medium-high speed until light and fluffy. Add the eggs and vanilla and beat 1 to 2 minutes until well mixed. Add the flour mixture alternately with water, beginning and ending with the flour mixture. Pour the batter into the pan.

**INTO THE OVEN** Bake for 45 to 55 minutes, until the cake springs back when lightly touched. Cool in the pan 10 minutes. Turn upside down onto a wire rack, remove the pan, and cool completely.

**FROST & DECORATE** Trim the top and edges of the cake. Draw a ghost shape on a 13 × 9-inch piece of waxed or parchment paper. Cut out the pattern and place it on top of the cake. Cut out the ghost-shaped cake and transfer to a large platter. Frost the top and sides of the cake. Decorate with the jelly beans for the eyes.

## Seven Minute Frosting

*Combine 1½ cups granulated sugar, ½ cup water, 2 large egg whites, 1 tablespoon light corn syrup, and ⅛ teaspoon salt in the top of a double boiler. Beat with an electric mixer on low speed for 1 minute. Place the double boiler over simmering water, increase the speed to high, and beat until stiff peaks form, about 7 minutes. Remove from the heat and add 1 teaspoon vanilla extract. Beat 2 to 3 minutes longer, until spreadable.*

    Makes 12 servings

    *Per serving: 474 calories, 5g protein, 82g carbohydrates, 16g fat, 8g saturated fat, 64mg cholesterol, 363mg sodium*

# Holiday Date Cake

*Prep* **15 minutes**   *Bake* **55 minutes + cooling**

- 2 cups all-purpose flour
- 1¼ teaspoons ground nutmeg
- 1¼ teaspoons baking soda
- 1 teaspoon baking powder
- ½ teaspoon salt
- ½ cup butter, softened
- 1¼ cups firmly packed dark brown sugar
- 3 large eggs
- 1 teaspoon vanilla extract
- 1 cup sour cream
- ¼ cup milk
- 1 cup chopped dates
- ½ cup chopped walnuts
- Confectioners' sugar (optional)
- Whipped cream (optional)

*Set the holidays in motion with our date-and-walnut-filled sour cream cake. Baking it in a Bundt pan guarantees that every slice will be pretty. Serve whipped cream alongside.*

**LET'S BEGIN** Preheat the oven to 350°F. Generously grease a 12-cup Bundt cake pan. Combine the flour, nutmeg, baking soda, baking powder, and salt in a medium bowl.

**MIX IT UP** Beat the butter and brown sugar in a large bowl with an electric mixer on medium-high speed until light and fluffy. Beat in the eggs, one at a time, beating well after each addition. Beat in the vanilla. Reduce the speed to low, add the flour mixture alternately with the sour cream and milk, beginning and ending with the flour mixture. Stir in the dates and walnuts. Pour the batter into the pan.

**INTO THE OVEN** Bake for 55 minutes, until a wooden toothpick inserted in the center comes out clean. Cool in the pan for 15 minutes. Turn upside down onto a wire rack and remove the pan. Cool completely. Dust with confectioners' sugar and serve with whipped cream, if you wish.

*Makes 16 servings*

*Per serving: 275 calories, 4g protein, 38g carbohydrates, 12g fat, 5g saturated fat, 61mg cholesterol, 258mg sodium*

---

### Time Savers

#### SPLITTING CAKE LAYERS FAST

Split cake layers fast, without using a knife. First mark the middle of one cake layer at 4-inch intervals with toothpicks. Cut a 3-foot-long piece of dental floss. Loop it around the cake by resting it on the toothpicks.

Now cross the ends of the floss, holding them in your hands, and pull the floss toward you, until the cake splits into two even layers.

# Plantation Pound Cake

*Prep* **20 minutes**   *Bake* **1 hour + cooling**

- 1¾ cups all-purpose flour
- 1 teaspoon grated lemon peel
- ¾ teaspoon baking soda
- ½ teaspoon salt (optional)
- ½ cup butter, softened
- 1 cup granulated sugar
- 4 large eggs
- ½ cup reduced-fat sour cream
- 1 teaspoon lemon juice
- 1 cup ground nuts
- Prepared frosting or confectioners' sugar

*Mix up a cooling pitcher of minted iced tea, pile thick slices of this rich and delicious nut-laden dessert on your favorite cake plate, and gather up some cozy chairs on your front porch. What better way to enjoy a lazy summer afternoon with friends?*

**LET'S BEGIN** Preheat the oven to 325°F. Grease and flour a 9 × 5-inch loaf pan. Combine the flour, lemon peel, baking soda, and salt, if desired, in a medium bowl. Set aside.

**BEAT & SWIRL** Beat the butter and granulated sugar in a large bowl with an electric mixer on medium speed until light and fluffy. Beat in the eggs, one at a time, beating well after each addition. Beat in the sour cream and lemon juice until blended. Reduce the speed to low, beat in the flour mixture, ½ cup at a time, just until blended. Pour half the batter into the pan. Sprinkle with the nuts. Top with the remaining batter. Gently swirl a narrow metal spatula or knife through the batter to marbleize.

**INTO THE OVEN** Bake for 60 to 70 minutes, until a wooden toothpick inserted in the center comes out clean. Cool the cake in the pan for 10 minutes. Unmold onto a wire rack, invert the cake right side up, and cool completely. Frost the cake with your choice of frostings or dust with confectioners' sugar.

**Makes 8 servings**

*Per serving: 788 calories, 9g protein, 105g carbohydrates, 39g total fat, 15g saturated fat, 39mg cholesterol, 336mg sodium*

# Merry Meringue Cake

*Prep* **15 minutes**   *Bake* **25 minutes**

- 4 large eggs, separated
- ½ teaspoon cream of tartar
- 1¼ cups sugar
- 1 cup all-purpose flour
- 1 teaspoon baking powder
- ¼ teaspoon salt
- ½ cup butter, softened
- ¼ cup milk
- 1 tablespoon lemon juice
- 2 teaspoons grated lemon zest

*Try using an egg separator so the yolks don't mix with the whites.*

**LET'S BEGIN** Preheat the oven to 350°F. Line the bottoms of two 8-inch round cake pans with waxed paper. To make the meringue, beat the egg whites and cream of tartar in a medium bowl with an electric mixer on high speed until foamy. Gradually add ¾ cup of the sugar, 2 tablespoons at a time, until the sugar is dissolved and the whites are glossy and stand in soft peaks. Set aside.

**MIX IT UP** Combine the flour, baking powder, and salt in a small bowl. Beat the butter and the remaining ½ cup sugar in a large bowl with an electric mixer on medium speed until light and fluffy. Blend in the egg yolks. Add the flour mixture alternately with the milk, beginning and ending with the flour mixture. Beat in the lemon juice and zest. Pour the batter into the pans. Spread the meringue over the batter in each pan, gently smoothing the tops.

**INTO THE OVEN** Bake for 25 minutes. Turn off the oven. Let the cakes stand in the oven for 5 minutes, then transfer to wire racks to cool for 10 minutes. Turn out onto racks, invert right side up, and cool completely. To serve, stack the layers on a plate (or serve as single layer cakes).

*Makes 8 servings*

*Per serving: 323 calories, 5g protein, 44g carbohydrates, 14g fat, 7g saturated fat, 138mg cholesterol, 286mg sodium*

## Baking Basics

### 7 WAYS TO AVOID WEEPING MERINGUE

Here are some tips for blue ribbon meringues from the pros:
- Make sure the piecrust doesn't contain any cracks.
- Be sure to add the sugar to the beaten egg whites gradually—only about 2 tablespoons at a time.
- Use superfine sugar, as it dissolves instantly. Or finely grind regular sugar in your food processor.
- Rub a small amount of whipped meringue between your fingers to make sure the sugar is all dissolved.
- Don't overbeat the egg whites. They should form stiff, glossy peaks that are very smooth—not clumpy or broken.
- Completely cover the pie filling with meringue. It should touch the crust edge all around.
- Cool the pie away from drafts.

# Chocolate Cherry Valentine

*Prep* **35 minutes**    *Bake* **18 minutes + cooling + decorating**

| | |
|---|---|
| 2 | large eggs, separated |
| 1½ | cups sugar |
| 1¼ | cups all-purpose flour |
| ½ | cup unsweetened cocoa |
| ¾ | teaspoon baking soda |
| ½ | teaspoon salt |
| 1 | cup buttermilk or sour milk (see page 110) |
| ½ | cup vegetable oil |
| 1 | can (21 ounces) cherry pie filling, chilled |

**Vanilla Cream Filling (see recipe)**

**Chocolate Whipped Cream (see recipe)**

*Let that special someone in your life know how much you love them by serving this beautiful 3-layered heart-shaped chocolate cake. If you only have 2 cake pans, don't worry—specific instructions with you in mind are included.*

**LET'S BEGIN** Preheat the oven to 350°F. Grease and flour three 9-inch heart-shaped baking pans or three 9-inch round cake pans. Beat the egg whites in a small bowl with an electric mixer until foamy. Gradually beat in ½ cup of the sugar, 1 tablespoon at a time, and beat until stiff peaks form. Set aside. Combine the flour, cocoa, baking soda, salt, and the remaining 1 cup sugar in a large bowl. Beat in the buttermilk, oil, and egg yolks with an electric mixer until smooth. Gently fold the beaten whites into the batter. Pour about 1⅔ cups batter into each pan. (If only 2 pans are available, reserve the remaining batter for the third layer in the refrigerator while the first 2 layers bake.)

**INTO THE OVEN** Bake for 18 to 20 minutes, until the cake springs back when lightly touched in the center. Cool in the pans 5 minutes. Unmold onto wire racks and cool completely. (Bake the third cake layer, if necessary.)

**FILL & FROST** Make the Vanilla Cream Filling. Place 1 cake layer on a serving plate and spoon a 1-inch border of the filling around the outer edge of the layer. Spread half the cherry pie filling in the center. Top with the second cake layer. Spread the top with half the remaining filling. Top with the third layer. Spoon the remaining cherry pie filling on top of this layer to within 1 inch of the edge. Spoon the remaining filling into a pastry bag fitted with a star tip. Pipe decoratively around the edge of the cherry pie filling. Make the Chocolate Whipped Cream and use to frost the sides of the cake. Refrigerate until ready to serve.

## Vanilla Cream Filling

Combine 1 cup cold heavy cream, 2 tablespoons sugar, and 1 teaspoon vanilla extract in a large bowl. Using an electric mixer, beat on low speed until blended. Increase the speed to high and beat until stiff.

## Chocolate Whipped Cream

Combine ½ cup sugar and ¼ cup unsweetened cocoa in a large bowl. Add 1 cup cold heavy cream and 1 teaspoon vanilla extract. Using an electric mixer, beat on low speed until blended. Increase the speed to high and beat until stiff.

Makes 8 servings

Per serving: 732 calories, 8g protein, 94g carbohydrates, 39g fat, 17g saturated fat, 136mg cholesterol, 351mg sodium

### Baking Basics

**4 FAST ICING TIPS**

When frosting cake layers:

- Freeze the layers for an hour (on a wire rack or on waxed paper). Then frost immediately. The layers will be easier to handle and stack while still slightly frozen. Usually, they are thawed by the time the cake is completely iced.
- Melt some jelly over low heat or in the microwave. Then gently brush a thin coating over the sides of the cake layers to keep crumbs out of the icing. You'll need about 1 cup of jelly (a 12-ounce jar) for a three-layer cake. Let the jelly dry for about 30 minutes before icing.
- Use a pastry scraper to pick up and spread a large amount of icing over the layers and around the sides fast—in just one or two strokes.
- Fit a pastry frosting bag with a cake icer tip (the large tip with a wide, flat opening). Fill with frosting and quickly pipe wide, thick rings around the top and sides of the cake. Spread smooth with a large flat metal spatula.

*Favorite Chocolate Cake, page 128*

# For the Crowd

When it comes to feeding a crowd, nothing is easier than baking a cake! There are lots to choose from: a rectangular chocolate picnic cake, an old-fashioned 1-2-3-4 butter cake with a rich fudge frosting, and one of those poppy seed cakes that has taken home so many blue ribbons. There's even a frosted cake you can take to a picnic. Each cake in this collection serves at least 12 hungry folks. That's a lot of cake! When you're cooking for a crowd, the cutting and serving are almost as important as the baking, so there are also tips on removing a cake from the pan—without losing a crumb—and keeping the cake fresh when baking it ahead. Your friends and family will love you!

# Apple Cinnamon Pecan Cake

*Prep* **25 minutes**  *Bake* **40 minutes + cooling**

- 2 cups all-purpose flour
- 2 teaspoons baking powder
- 1 teaspoon ground cinnamon
- ½ teaspoon ground nutmeg
- 1 cup granulated sugar
- ½ cup butter, softened
- 2 large eggs
- 1 teaspoon vanilla extract
- 1 can (5 ounces) evaporated low-fat milk
- 3 cups peeled and finely chopped baking apples
- ¾ cup pecans, finely chopped
- Confectioners' sugar

*Serve this excellent cake as an after-school treat with cold milk or enjoy it as a mid-morning snack with a steaming cup of coffee.*

**LET'S BEGIN** Preheat the oven to 350°F. Grease a 13 × 9-inch baking pan.

**MIX IT UP** Combine the flour, baking powder, cinnamon, and nutmeg in a medium bowl. Beat the granulated sugar and butter in a large bowl with an electric mixer until creamy. Beat in the eggs and vanilla until smooth. Beat in the flour mixture alternately with the evaporated milk, beginning and ending with the flour mixture. Stir in the apples and pecans. Spread the batter into the pan.

**INTO THE OVEN** Bake for 40 to 45 minutes, until a wooden toothpick inserted in the center comes out clean. Cool in the pan on a wire rack for 20 minutes. Cut into bars. Sprinkle with confectioners' sugar before serving.

*Makes 15 servings*

*Per serving: 240 calories, 3g protein, 31g carbohydrates, 11g fat, 4g saturated fat, 46mg cholesterol, 91mg sodium*

---

## Time Savers

### 6 EASY RULES FOR CUTTING THE CAKE—FAST!

When the crowd is waiting for you to cut the cake, you need all the tips you can get! Here are a few to help keep the crumbs from flying and keep the icing on each slice.

- Chill the cake layers before you ice them. This firms them up and makes them easier to slice.
- Choose an icing that sets at room temperature. Ideally, it will be somewhat firm to the touch—but not dry or crumbly.
- If you're baking and icing the cake the day before serving, let it come back to room temperature before cutting. Remember: Versatile buttercream frosting is mostly butter, which hardens in the refrigerator. If you try to slice it cold, it can easily tear the cake.
- Use a serrated knife for slicing butter cakes.
- Use a cake breaker (the one with long, thin prongs) for slicing (or "breaking") foam cakes, such as angel food, chiffon, or sponge.
- Keep a pitcher of hot water handy. Occasionally, dip the knife into the water to warm and clean it at the same time.

# Favorite Chocolate Cake

*Prep* **20 minutes**   *Bake* **30 minutes + cooling**

| | |
|---|---|
| 4 | ounces unsweetened baking chocolate, broken into pieces |
| ½ | cup butter or margarine |
| 2 | cups sugar |
| 2 | cups all-purpose flour |
| 1 | cup milk |
| ½ | cup water |
| 2 | large eggs |
| 1 | tablespoon lemon juice or white distilled vinegar |
| 1 | teaspoon vanilla extract |
| 1 | teaspoon baking powder |
| 1 | teaspoon baking soda |
| ¼ | teaspoon salt |
| ½ | cup water |
| Prepared chocolate frosting (optional) | |

*This cake may very well become your most favorite. It has lots of chocolate flavor, is nice and moist, and takes only minutes to get into the oven. What more could one want?*

**LET'S BEGIN** Grease and flour two 9-inch round cake pans. Place the chocolate in a microwaveable bowl. Microwave on High for 1 minute and stir just until melted and smooth. (If necessary, microwave at additional 10- to 15-second intervals until smooth.) Cool to room temperature.

**MIX IT UP** Meanwhile, preheat the oven to 350°F. Beat the butter and sugar in a large bowl with an electric mixer on medium-high speed until well blended. Reduce the speed to low, beat in the flour, milk, water, eggs, lemon juice, vanilla, baking powder, baking soda, and salt just until blended. Increase the speed to high and beat for 2 minutes. Beat in the melted chocolate. Pour the batter into the pans.

**INTO THE OVEN** Bake for 30 to 35 minutes, until a wooden toothpick inserted in the center comes out clean. Cool in the pans for 20 minutes. Invert onto wire racks, remove the pans and cool completely. Frost and fill the cake with chocolate frosting, if you wish.

*Makes 18 servings*

*Per serving: 230 calories, 3g protein, 35g carbohydrates, 10g fat, 5g saturated fat, 39mg cholesterol, 170mg sodium*

# MAPLE WALNUT POUND CAKE

*Prep* **20 MINUTES**     *Bake* **1 HOUR + COOLING**

- 2¼ cups all-purpose flour
- 1 teaspoon baking powder
- ½ teaspoon salt
- ¼ cup milk
- 1 tablespoon maple flavoring
- 1 cup butter or margarine, softened
- 1½ cups granulated sugar
- ½ cup firmly packed brown sugar
- 5 large eggs
- 1½ cups walnuts, chopped

**MAPLE GLAZE**

- 1 cup sifted confectioners' sugar
- 1 to 1½ tablespoons milk
- ¼ teaspoon maple flavoring
- Walnut halves or chopped walnuts, for garnish

*Just a little bit of maple flavoring (available in the baking section in supermarkets) goes a long way to flavoring up this ever-so-delectable pound cake. Did you know that pound cakes originally got their name because they were made with 1 pound each of flour, butter, sugar, and eggs?*

**LET'S BEGIN** Preheat the oven to 300°F. Grease a 9- or 10-inch tube pan. Combine the flour, baking powder, and salt in a medium bowl. Combine the milk and maple flavoring in a glass measure. Beat the butter, granulated sugar, and brown sugar in a large bowl with an electric mixer on medium-high speed until light and fluffy. Reduce the speed to low, add the flour mixture alternately with the milk mixture, beginning and ending with the flour mixture. Add the eggs, one at a time, beating well after each addition. Stir in the walnuts. Pour the batter into the pan.

**INTO THE OVEN** Bake in the lower third of the oven for 60 to 75 minutes, until a wooden toothpick inserted in the center comes out clean. Cool in the pan for 15 minutes. Turn upside down onto a wire rack and remove the pan. Cool completely.

**GLAZE IT** To make the maple glaze, whisk the confectioners' sugar with enough of the milk until the mixture is thick and pourable. Whisk in the maple flavoring. Drizzle the glaze over the cake, garnish with the walnuts, if you wish. Let the cake stand until the glaze is set.

**Makes 12 servings**

*Per serving: 525 calories, 8g protein, 62g carbohydrates, 29g fat, 10g saturated fat, 132mg cholesterol, 270mg sodium*

# Mile-High Almond Cake

*Prep* **20 minutes**   *Bake* **1 hour + cooling**

| | |
|---|---|
| 4 | large eggs, separated |
| 2½ | cups granulated sugar |
| 4 | cups cake flour (not self-rising) |
| 2 | tablespoons baking powder |
| 1 | teaspoon salt |
| 2 | cups milk |
| 1 | cup almond oil |
| 1½ | teaspoons almond extract |
| 1½ | teaspoons vanilla extract |

Almond Glaze (see recipe)

*This is a fabulous cake for company, as it makes a generous 16 servings, and is delicious as is or with a big bowl of whipped cream.*

**LET'S BEGIN** Preheat oven to 350°F. Beat egg whites in a large bowl with an electric mixer on high speed until frothy. Gradually add ½ cup of the granulated sugar, beating well until stiff peaks form. Set aside.

**MIX IT UP** Combine the cake flour, baking powder, salt, and remaining 2 cups sugar in a large bowl. Add the egg yolks, milk, almond oil, almond extract, and vanilla. Beat with an electric mixer on medium speed for 3 minutes, scraping the bottom and sides of the bowl often, until smooth. With a rubber spatula, gently fold half of the beaten whites into the batter. Repeat with the remaining whites just until blended. Pour the batter into an ungreased 10-inch tube pan.

**INTO THE OVEN** Bake for 60 to 65 minutes, until a wooden toothpick inserted halfway between the tube and side of the pan comes out clean. Cool in the pan for 15 minutes. Run a metal spatula or knife around the sides of the pan and tube. Lift the tube and cake out and cool the cake completely. Invert the cake onto a wire rack and remove the bottom of the pan. Invert again right side up onto a serving plate. Make the Almond Glaze and drizzle it over the top of cake, letting it run down the sides.

## Almond Glaze

Combine 1 cup sifted confectioners' sugar, 1½ tablespoons milk, 1 tablespoon almond oil, and ¼ teaspoon almond extract in a large bowl. Whisk until smooth.

**Makes 16 servings**

*Per serving: 410 calories, 5g protein, 59g carbohydrates, 17g fat, 2g saturated fat, 56mg cholesterol, 267mg sodium*

# Patriot Cake

Prep **25 MINUTES + DECORATING**  Bake **35 MINUTES**

- 2 boxes (14 ounces each) pound cake mix, or 2 packages (18.25 ounces each) any cake mix (following the directions for making a pound cake)
- 2 tubs (16 ounces each) vanilla frosting
- Blue food coloring
- 1 package (14 ounces) red, white, and blue milk or peanut candy-coated chocolate candies

*Here is the perfect cake for celebrating your next Fourth of July. The cake is super-easy to bake and decorate into the most spectacular American flag ever.*

**LET'S BEGIN** Preheat the oven to 350°F. Prepare the two boxes of the cake mix according to package directions. Pour the batter into two 13 × 9-inch nonstick baking pans. Bake the cakes for 35 to 40 minutes, until the sides of the cakes pull away from the sides of the pans. Let cool for 10 minutes in the pans. Turn each cake upside down onto a wire rack, remove the pans, and cool completely.

**CUT & FROST** Cut 1 of the cakes into 2 different sizes, a 7 × 5-inch rectangle and a 9 × 7-inch rectangle (leave the other cake uncut). Spoon one-quarter of the frosting into a bowl and add enough blue food coloring to tint the frosting a vibrant blue. Spoon the blue frosting into a resealable plastic bag. Set aside. Frost the cake layers with the remaining white frosting. Beginning with the largest cake, stack them from the largest to smallest. For the blue part of the flag, snip one corner of the plastic bag and pipe a rectangle in the top left corner of the smallest cake layer. Pipe part of a rectangle in the top left corner of the remaining layers. Fill in the corners by squeezing the remaining blue frosting from the bag, then spreading it smooth with the back of a spoon or table knife.

**STARS & STRIPES** To make the stars, arrange white chocolate candies in straight parallel lines, covering the blue area of the cake. To make the stripes, arrange straight parallel lines with red chocolate candies across the white area of the cake.

*Makes 24 servings*
Per serving: 411 calories, 3g protein, 77g carbohydrates, 10g fat, 4g saturated fat, 38mg cholesterol, 155mg sodium

# 1-2-3-4 Butter Cake

*Prep* **25 MINUTES**   *Bake* **45 MINUTES**

## CAKE

- 3 cups all-purpose flour
- 2 teaspoons baking powder
- ½ teaspoon salt
- 2 cups granulated sugar
- 1 cup butter, softened
- 4 large eggs
- 2 teaspoons vanilla extract
- 1 cup milk

## CHOCOLATE BUTTER FROSTING

- ½ cup butter, softened
- 3 squares (3 ounces) unsweetened baking chocolate, melted and cooled
- 4 cups confectioners' sugar
- ¼ cup milk
- 2 teaspoons vanilla extract
- Decorator sprinkles (optional)

*When you want something simple—and simply delicious—this is it? Chances are your grandmother even made this cake, as it's been an American favorite for generations.*

**LET'S BEGIN** Preheat the oven to 350°F. Grease a 13 × 9-inch baking pan. To make the cake, combine the flour, baking powder, and salt in a medium bowl. Beat the granulated sugar and butter in a large bowl with an electric mixer on medium speed, scraping the bowl occasionally, until creamy. Add the eggs, two at a time, beating well after each addition. Add the vanilla. Reduce the speed to low and add the flour mixture alternately with the milk, beginning and ending with the flour mixture and beating well after each addition. Pour the batter into the pan.

**INTO THE OVEN** Bake for 45 to 55 minutes, until a wooden toothpick inserted in the center comes out clean. Transfer to a wire rack and cool completely.

**FROST IT** To make the frosting, beat the butter and chocolate in a large bowl with an electric mixer on medium speed until creamy. Gradually add the confectioners' sugar, alternately with the milk and vanilla, scraping the bowl occasionally, until well mixed. Frost the top of the cake. Sprinkle with decorator sprinkles, if desired.

*Makes 15 servings*

*Per serving: 490 calories, 5g protein, 74g carbohydrates, 20g fat, 10g saturated fat, 105mg cholesterol, 320mg sodium*

# Baking Basics

## BUTTER CAKE FIX-IT TIPS

So your butter cake didn't turn out exactly perfect? Review these fix-it tips to know what to do better the next time you bake a butter cake.

**If the cake didn't rise enough:**
- Check to see that your baking powder and baking soda are fresh and that you didn't use more than the recipe called for.
- Put the cake into a preheated oven as soon as the batter is stirred up. Baking powder and baking soda begin working the minute they come in contact with liquid, so the faster the cake gets into the oven, the higher it'll rise.
- Cream the butter and sugar well, until it looks light and fluffy. This incorporates extra air, which helps the cake to rise high. If the batter doesn't look fluffy, keep mixing!
- Wait until the butter and eggs are at room temperature before using (this usually takes at least 30 to 45 minutes).

**If the cake was so dry it crumbled and fell apart when you tried to remove it from the pan, ice it, or cut it, chances are:**
- You overmixed the batter after adding the flour. Next time, mix the batter only until the white flour disappears—no longer.
- The pans weren't greased enough. Next time, use plenty of butter or shortening, be sure you coat both the sides and the bottom of the pan well, and dust with a little flour. Cut out circles of parchment paper to line the bottoms of the pans.
- The cake didn't cool enough before you took it out of the pan.

**If the cake sinks after a few minutes out of the oven:**
Chances are the cake wasn't done. Even in the best ovens, temperatures vary. So always use an oven thermometer. And before taking out the cake, wait until a wooden toothpick you insert in the center comes out dry or the cake springs back when lightly touched in the center.

FOR THE CROWD

# Orange Rum Savarin

*Prep* **20 minutes + rising**   *Bake* **20 minutes + cooling**

| | |
|---|---|
| 2 | cups all-purpose flour |
| 1¼ | cups sugar |
| 1 | package active dry yeast |
| ½ | teaspoon salt |
| ½ | cup butter, cut into pieces |
| ⅓ | cup skim or low-fat milk |
| 6 | large eggs |
| ¾ | cup raisins or currants |
| ½ | cup chopped nuts |
| ½ | cup orange juice |
| ½ | teaspoon rum flavoring |

*A savarin is a cake made from a buttery yeast batter that is soaked with a flavored sugar syrup. Most savarins are baked in a ring mold; using a fluted tube pan makes this one lovely to look at.*

**LET'S BEGIN** Combine the flour, ¼ cup of the sugar, yeast, and salt in a large bowl of a heavy-duty mixer. Heat the butter and milk in a small saucepan over medium heat, until hot (120° to 130°F). Add to the flour mixture. Add the eggs, one at a time, beating with a paddle attachment on low speed until blended. Increase the speed to high and beat 3 minutes. Stir in the raisins and nuts.

**RISE & BAKE** Cover the bowl with plastic wrap and let the dough rise in a warm, draft-free place until doubled in size, 1 to 1½ hours. Stir down the dough. Spoon into a greased 9-cup fluted tube pan. Cover and let rise in a warm place until doubled, about 45 minutes.

**INTO THE OVEN** Meanwhile, preheat the oven to 350°F. Bake the dough for 20 to 25 minutes, until lightly browned and a wooden toothpick inserted near the center comes out clean. Cool in the pan for 10 minutes. Turn upside down onto a serving plate and remove the pan.

**MAKE SYRUP** Meanwhile, combine the orange juice and the remaining 1 cup sugar in a small saucepan. Cook over medium-high heat, stirring constantly, until the mixture boils. Remove from the heat. Stir in the rum flavoring. With the tines of a fork, pierce the warm savarin at 1-inch intervals. Slowly spoon the syrup over the savarin until it is absorbed. Cool completely.

*Makes 12 servings*

*Per serving: 331 calories, 7g protein, 46g carbohydrates, 14g fat, 5g saturated fat, 127mg cholesterol, 194mg sodium*

# Orange Honey Sponge Cake

*Prep* **25 minutes**   *Bake* **45 minutes + cooling**

- 1¼ cups all-purpose flour
- 1 tablespoon grated orange peel
- 1½ teaspoons baking powder
- ¼ teaspoon salt
- 6 large eggs, separated
- ½ cup sugar
- ½ cup honey
- 2 tablespoons orange juice
- Honey Whipped Cream (see recipe)
- Grated orange zest (optional)

*This light and airy orange-flavored sponge cake has honey to thank for its unique flavor and moist texture. Adding a small amount of honey to whipped cream is an easy way to make it special.*

**LET'S BEGIN** Preheat the oven to 350°F. Combine the flour, orange peel, baking powder, and salt in a medium bowl. Beat the egg yolks in a large bowl with an electric mixer on medium-high speed until very light. Gradually beat in the sugar, 1 tablespoon at a time, until thick and lemon-colored. Beat in the honey and orange juice until blended. Reduce the speed to low and gradually blend in the flour mixture.

**MIX IT UP** Beat the egg whites in another large bowl with an electric mixer until stiff but not dry. With a rubber spatula, gently fold one-third of the whites into the batter. Repeat twice more with the remaining whites just until blended. (Do not overmix.) Pour the batter into an ungreased 9-inch tube pan.

**BAKE & DECORATE** Bake for 45 to 50 minutes, until the cake springs back when lightly touched. Immediately invert the pan onto a funnel or bottle. Cool completely. Run a metal spatula or knife around the sides of the pan and tube. Invert the cake onto a serving plate. Make the Honey Whipped Cream and put some of it in a pastry bag fitted with a star tip. Pipe along the outer edge of top of cake. Garnish with the orange zest, if you wish. Serve with rest of whipped cream.

## Honey Whipped Cream

*Beat 1 cup heavy cream in a large bowl with an electric mixer on high until thickened. Gradually add 3 tablespoons honey and beat until soft peaks form. Fold in 1 teaspoon vanilla extract.*

*Makes 12 servings (including whipped cream)*
*Per serving: 259 calories, 5g protein, 35g carbohydrates, 11g fat, 6g saturated fat, 137mg cholesterol, 127mg sodium*

# LEMON POPPYSEED CAKE

*Prep* **15 MINUTES**   *Bake* **1 HOUR + COOLING**

- 3 cups all-purpose flour
- ¼ teaspoon baking soda
- 1 cup butter or margarine, softened
- 2 cups granulated sugar
- 4 large eggs
- 1 cup sour cream
- 2 tablespoons poppy seeds
- 2 teaspoons lemon extract
- 1 teaspoon vanilla extract
- 1 teaspoon grated lemon peel

**LEMON GLAZE**

- 1½ cups confectioners' sugar
- ½ teaspoon lemon extract
- 2 tablespoons + 1 teaspoon water
- Fresh fruit or berries

*Lemon poppy seed cake has become an American classic and for good reason—it's delicious and easy. A double dose of lemon from tasty lemon extract and fresh lemon peel make this cake a real keeper. To ensure freshness, store poppy seeds in the refrigerator so they don't turn rancid.*

**LET'S BEGIN** Preheat the oven to 325°F. Grease a 12-cup Bundt cake pan. Combine the flour and baking soda in a medium bowl. Beat the butter in a large bowl with an electric mixer on medium-high speed until creamy. Gradually beat in the sugar. Add the eggs, one at a time, beating well after each addition. Reduce the speed to low, beat in half the flour mixture. Add the sour cream, then beat in the remaining flour mixture. Stir in the poppy seeds, lemon extract, vanilla, and lemon peel. Spoon the batter into the pan.

**INTO THE OVEN** Bake for 60 to 65 minutes, until a wooden toothpick inserted in the center comes out clean. Cool in the pan for 15 minutes. Turn upside down onto a wire rack and remove the pan. Cool completely.

**GLAZE IT** To make the lemon glaze, whisk the confectioners' sugar, water, and lemon extract in a small bowl until smooth. Spoon the glaze over the cake, letting the excess drip down the sides. Let the cake stand until the glaze is set. Serve with fresh fruit or berries.

*Makes 20 servings*

*Per serving: 306 calories, 4g protein, 43g carbohydrates, 13g fat, 7g saturated fat, 73mg cholesterol, 133mg sodium*

# Banana Jewel Cake

*Prep* **15 MINUTES**  *Bake* **35 MINUTES + COOLING**

| | |
|---|---|
| 1 | package (18.25 ounces) vanilla or white cake mix |
| ¼ | cup orange juice |
| ¼ | cup sugar |
| 2 | tablespoons grated orange zest |
| 1½ | cups fresh cranberries |
| 3 | ripe bananas, sliced |

With a cake mix and a few other ingredients, you are well on your way to a special cake. If using fresh-squeezed orange juice, be sure to grate the oranges before you juice them; it's so much easier. And don't forget to wash the oranges first.

**LET'S BEGIN** Preheat the oven to 350°F. Prepare the cake mix according to package directions, except add only 1 cup water. Pour into a 13 × 9-inch baking pan.

**TOP IT** Combine the orange juice, sugar, and orange zest in a medium saucepan and bring to a simmer, stirring to dissolve the sugar. Add the cranberries and simmer until the skins burst. Stir in the bananas and cook 1 minute longer. Remove from the heat. Evenly spoon the cranberry-banana mixture over the batter in the pan. Do not stir.

**INTO THE OVEN** Bake for 35 to 40 minutes until lightly browned. Transfer to a wire rack and cool completely.

*Makes 12 servings*

Per serving: 232 calories, 1g protein, 48g carbohydrates, 4g fat, 2g saturated fat, 0mg cholesterol, 251mg sodium

# TAKE-ME-TO-A-PICNIC CAKE

*Prep* **25 MINUTES**  *Bake* **25 MINUTES + COOLING**

- 1 cup water
- 1 cup butter or margarine, cut up
- ½ cup unsweetened cocoa
- 2 cups sugar
- 1¾ cups all-purpose flour
- 1 teaspoon baking soda
- ½ teaspoon salt
- 3 large eggs
- ¾ cup sour cream
- Peanut Butter Chip Frosting (see recipe)
- Chocolate Garnish (optional, see recipe)

*Don't even think of leaving out the small amount of vegetable shortening in the chocolate garnish. It adds just the right amount of shine and easy-to-use texture to the melted chocolate chips.*

**LET'S BEGIN** Preheat the oven to 350°F. Grease and flour a 15½ × 10½-inch jelly-roll pan. Bring the first 3 ingredients to a boil over medium heat, stirring. Boil 1 minute. Remove from the heat and set aside.

**MIX IT UP** Stir the sugar, flour, baking soda, and salt together in a large bowl. Add eggs and sour cream; beat with an electric mixer until blended. Add cocoa mixture and beat just until blended (the batter will be thin). Pour into the pan.

**BAKE & FROST** Bake for 25 to 30 minutes, or until a wooden toothpick inserted in the center comes out clean. Transfer the cake to a wire rack and cool completely. Meanwhile, make the Peanut Butter Chip Frosting and spread it over the top of the cake. If you wish, make the Chocolate Garnish to drizzle over the frosting.

## PEANUT BUTTER CHIP FROSTING

*Combine ⅓ cup butter or margarine, ⅓ cup milk, and one 10-ounce package peanut butter chips in a medium saucepan. Cook over low heat, stirring constantly, until the chips are melted and the mixture is smooth. Remove from the heat and stir in 1 teaspoon vanilla extract. Place 1 cup confectioners' sugar in a medium bowl. Gradually beat in the chip mixture until well blended.*

## CHOCOLATE GARNISH

Combine ½ cup semisweet chocolate chips and 1 teaspoon vegetable shortening in a small microwaveable bowl and microwave on High 1 for minute (do not use butter, margarine, spread, or oil). Stir until the chips are melted and the mixture is smooth.

**Makes 20 servings**
Per serving: 384 calories, 6g protein, 45g carbohydrates, 21g fat, 13g saturated fat, 70mg cholesterol, 264mg sodium

# CREDITS

**PAGE 2** Land O'Lakes: Photo for 1-2-3-4 Butter Cake courtesy of Land O'Lakes, Inc. Used with permission.

**PAGE 8** Land O'Lakes: Photo for Blue Ribbon Apple Pie courtesy of Land O'Lakes, Inc. Used with permission.

**PAGE 13** Kraft Foods: Photo for Brownie Bottom Pudding Pie courtesy of Kraft Kitchens. Used with permission.

**PAGE 16** McCormick: Photo for Cinnamon Raisin Cake courtesy of McCormick. Used with permission.

**PAGE 18** California Strawberry Commission: Recipe for Classic Strawberry Shortcake courtesy of © California Strawberry Commission. All rights reserved. Used with permission.

**PAGE 19** California Strawberry Commission: Recipe for Strawberry Angel Shortcakes courtesy of the © California Strawberry Commission. All rights reserved. Used with permission.

**PAGES 20/21** Land O'Lakes: Photo and recipe for Berry Sour Cream Shortcake courtesy of Land O'Lakes, Inc. Used with permission.

**PAGE 22** Land O'Lakes: Recipe for Buttery Pound Cake courtesy of Land O'Lakes, Inc. Used with permission.

**PAGE 23** Cherry Marketing Institute: Recipe for Cherry-Mallow Cake courtesy of The Cherry Marketing Institute. Used with permission.

**PAGE 24** Dole: Recipe for Fabulous Carrot Cake courtesy of Dole Food Company. Used with permission.

**PAGE 25** McCormick: Recipe for Cinnamon Raisin Cake courtesy of McCormick. Used with permission.

**PAGE 26** Bird's Eye Foods: Recipe for Apple Cinnamon Cake courtesy of Bird's Eye Foods. Used with permission.

**PAGE 27** Haagen-Dazs: Recipe for Ice Cream Cake Roll courtesy of Dreyer's Grand Ice Cream, Inc. Used with permission.

**PAGES 28/29** Land O'Lakes: Photo and recipe for Pineapple Upside-Down Cake courtesy of Land O'Lakes, Inc. Used with permission.

**PAGE 30** McCormick: Recipe for Light Spice Cupcakes courtesy of McCormick. Used with permission.

**PAGE 31** Sugar in the Raw: Recipe for Banana Cake courtesy of Claudia Fleming, Pastry Chef, Gramercy Tavern, NYC.

**PAGE 32** Nestlé: Recipe for Extreme Banana Cream Pie courtesy of Nestlé. All trademarks are owned by Société des Produits Nestlé S.A., Vevey, Switzerland. Used with permission.

**PAGE 33** Domino: Recipe for Classic Southern Pecan Pie courtesy of Domino Sugar. Used with permission.

**PAGE 34** Bird's Eye Foods: Recipe for Quick & Easy Fruit Cobbler courtesy of Birds Eye Foods. Used with permission.

**PAGE 35** Dole: Photo and recipe for Simply Good Cobbler courtesy of Dole Food Company. Used with permission.

**PAGE 36** Wisconsin Milk Marketing Board: Photo and recipe for Apple Colby Crisp courtesy of the Wisconsin Milk Marketing Board, Inc. Used with permission.

**PAGE 37** Del Monte: Recipe for Easy Peach Crisp courtesy of Del Monte Foods. Used with permission.

**PAGE 38** Domino: Recipe for Almond Crunch Snack Cake courtesy of Domino Sugar. Used with permission.

**PAGE 39** Nestlé: Photo and recipe for Chocolate Almond Coffee Cake courtesy of Nestlé. All trademarks are owned by Société des Produits Nestlé S.A., Vevey, Switzerland. Used with permission.

**PAGE 40** Nestlé: Photo for Chocoholic Cake courtesy of Nestlé. All trademarks are owned by Société des Produits Nestlé S.A., Vevey, Switzerland. Used with permission.

**PAGE 42** Tone Brothers: Recipe for Red Velvet Cake courtesy of Tone Brothers, Inc., producer of Tone's, Spice Islands, and Durkee products. Used with permission.

**PAGE 43** Nestlé: Recipe for Chocoholic Cake courtesy of Nestlé. All trademarks are owned by Société des Produits Nestlé S.A., Vevey, Switzerland. Used with permission.

**PAGE 44** Nestlé: Recipe for Chocolate Angel Food Cake courtesy of Nestlé. All trademarks are owned by Société des Produits Nestlé S.A., Vevey, Switzerland. Used with permission.

**PAGE 45** Kraft Foods: Recipe for Midnight Bliss courtesy of Kraft Kitchens. Used with permission.

**PAGES 46/47** National Honey Board: Photo and recipe for Mile High Chocolate Cake courtesy of the National Honey Board. Used with permission.

**PAGE 48** Ocean Spray Cranberries: Photo and recipe for Chocolate Volcano courtesy of Ocean Spray Cranberries, Inc. Used with permission.

**PAGE 49** Kraft Foods: Recipe for 3-Layer German Sweet Chocolate Cake courtesy of Kraft Kitchens. Used with permission.

**PAGE 50** Sargento: Recipe for Triple Chocolate Cheesecake courtesy of Sargento Foods, Inc. Used with permission.

**PAGE 51** Hershey: Recipe for Gone to Heaven Chocolate Pie courtesy of Hershey Kitchens, Hershey Foods Corporation, Hershey, PA. Used with permission.

**PAGE 52** Nestlé: Recipe for Chocolate Banana Cream Pie courtesy of Nestlé. All trademarks are owned by Société des Produits Nestlé S.A., Vevey, Switzerland. Used with permission.

**PAGE 53** Kraft Foods: Photo and recipe for Brownie Bottom Pudding Pie courtesy of Kraft Kitchens. Used with permission.

**PAGES 54/55** Kraft Foods: Photo and recipe for White Chocolate Coconut Cream Pie courtesy of Kraft Kitchens. Used with permission.

**PAGE 56** Hershey: Recipe for Chocolate Pecan Pie courtesy of Hershey Kitchens, Hershey Foods Corporation, Hershey, PA. Used with permission.

**PAGE 57** Hershey: Recipe for Dark Chocolate Layered Cheesecake courtesy of Hershey Kitchens, Hershey Foods Corporation, Hershey, PA. Used with permission.

**PAGE 58** Domino: Recipe for Easy Fudge Cake with Buttercream Frosting courtesy of Domino Sugar. Used with permission.

**PAGE 59** McCormick: Recipe for Black Forest Cake courtesy of McCormick. Used with permission.

**PAGES 60/61** Hershey: Photo and recipe for Heritage Chocolate Cake courtesy of Hershey Kitchens, Hershey Foods Corporation, Hershey, PA. Used with permission.

**PAGE 62** Hershey: Recipe for Special Dark Picnic Cake courtesy of Hershey Kitchens, Hershey Foods Corporation, Hershey, PA. Used with permission.

**PAGE 63** Tone Brothers: Recipe for Chocolate Espresso Fudge Cake courtesy of Tone Brothers, Inc., producer of Tone's, Spice Islands, and Durkee products. Used with permission.

**PAGE 64** Land O'Lakes: Photo for Candy 'n' Balloon Birthday Cake courtesy of Land O'Lakes, Inc. Used with permission.

**PAGES 66/67** Kraft Foods: Photo and recipe for Brownie Mud Puddle Cake courtesy of Kraft Kitchens. Used with permission.

**PAGE 68** Sugar in the Raw: Recipe for Sand Castle Cake courtesy of *Sugar in the Raw* turbinado sugar. Used with permission.

**PAGE 69** Sugar in the Raw: Recipe for Butterfly Cake courtesy of *Sugar in the Raw* turbinado sugar. Used with permission.

**PAGE 70** Land O'Lakes: Recipe for Candy 'n' Balloon Birthday Cake courtesy of Land O'Lakes, Inc. Used with permission.

**PAGE 71** Hershey: Recipe for Jack O' Lantern courtesy of Hershey Kitchens, Hershey Foods Corporation, Hershey, PA. Used with permission.

**PAGE 72** Kraft Foods: Recipe for Dinosaur Birthday Cake courtesy of Kraft Kitchens. Used with permission.

**PAGE 73** Kraft Foods: Recipe for Graveyard Pizza courtesy of Kraft Kitchens. Used with permission.

**PAGE 74** National Honey Board: Recipe for Honey-Almond Sweet Pizza courtesy of the National Honey Board. Used with permission.

**PAGE 74** Hershey: Recipe for S'more Cookie Bars courtesy of Hershey Kitchens, Hershey Foods Corporation, Hershey, PA. Used with permission.

**PAGE 75** Tone Brothers: Recipe for Bunny Cake courtesy of Tone Brothers, Inc., producer of Tone's, Spice Islands, and Durkee products. Used with permission.

**PAGE 76** Hershey: Photo and recipe for Winter Wonderland Snowmen courtesy of Hershey Kitchens, Hershey Foods Corporation, Hershey, PA. Used with permission.

**PAGE 76** McCormick: Recipe for Chocolate Chip Cookie Cake courtesy of McCormick. Used with permission.

**PAGE 78** Nestlé: Photo and recipe for Peanutty Goober Cake courtesy of Nestlé. All trademarks are owned by Société des Produits Nestlé S.A., Vevey, Switzerland. Used with permission.

**PAGE 79** Nestlé: Photo and recipe for Dalmatian Cupcakes courtesy of Nestlé. All trademarks are owned by Société des Produits Nestlé S.A., Vevey, Switzerland. Used with permission.

**PAGES 80/81** McCormick: Photo and recipe for Cupid's Cupcakes courtesy of McCormick. Used with permission.

**PAGE 82** Land O'Lakes: Photo for Holiday Fruited Pound Cake courtesy of Land O'Lakes, Inc. Used with permission.

**PAGE 84** Nestlé: Recipe for Tis Spring! Cheesecake courtesy of Nestlé. All trademarks are owned by Société des Produits Nestlé S.A., Vevey, Switzerland. Used with permission.

**PAGE 85** California Strawberry Commission: Photo and recipe for Strawberry Crown Tart courtesy of © California Strawberry Commission. All rights reserved. Used with permission.

**PAGE 86** American Egg Board: Photo and recipe for Strawberry Rhubarb Custard Pie courtesy of the American Egg Board. Used with permission.

**PAGE 76** Tone Brothers: Photo and recipe for Fresh Peach & Blueberry Pie courtesy of Tone Brothers, Inc., producer of Tone's, Spice Islands, and Durkee products. Used with permission.

**PAGE 88** Domino: Recipe for Fresh Blueberry Pie courtesy of Domino Sugar. Used with permission.

**PAGE 89** Cherry Marketing Institute: Photo and recipe for Dried Cherry Apple Pie courtesy of The Cherry Marketing Institute. Used with permission.

**PAGE 90** Sunkist: Recipe for Citrus Mini Tarts courtesy of Sunkist Growers, Inc. Used with permission.

**PAGE 91** Almond Board of California: Recipe for Almond & Mixed Berry Tart courtesy of the Almond Board of California. Used with permission.

**PAGE 92** Land O'Lakes: Recipe for Blue Ribbon Apple Pie courtesy of Land O'Lakes, Inc. Used with permission.

**PAGE 93** Nestlé: Photo and recipe for Famous Pumpkin Pie courtesy of Nestlé. All trademarks are owned by Société des Produits Nestlé S.A., Vevey, Switzerland. Used with permission.

**PAGE 94** National Honey Board: Recipe for Cranberry Pecan Pie courtesy of the National Honey Board. Used with permission.

**PAGE 95** Ocean Spray Cranberries. Photo and recipe for Rustic Cranberry Apple Tart courtesy of Ocean Spray Cranberries, Inc. Used with permission.

**PAGE 96** Haagen-Dazs: Recipe for Lemon Ribbon Ice Cream Pie courtesy of Dreyer's Grand Ice Cream, Inc. Used with permission.

**PAGE 97** Haagen-Dazs: Recipe for Frozen Key Lime Torte courtesy of

Dreyer's Grand Ice Cream, Inc. Used with permission.

PAGE 98 Kraft Foods: Recipe for Pumpkin Spice Cake courtesy of Kraft Kitchens. Used with permission.

PAGE 99 Ocean Spray Cranberries: Photo and recipe for Cranberry Pumpkin Cheesecake courtesy of Ocean Spray Cranberries, Inc. Used with permission.

PAGE 100 Wisconsin Milk Marketing Board: Recipe for Holiday Eggnog Cake courtesy of the Wisconsin Milk Marketing Board, Inc. Used with permission.

PAGE 101 Land O'Lakes: Recipe for Holiday Fruited Pound Cake courtesy of Land O'Lakes, Inc. Used with permission.

PAGE 102 American Egg Board: Photo for Merry Meringue Cake courtesy of the American Egg Board. Used with permission.

PAGES 104/105 Land O'Lakes: Photo and recipe for Birthday Cake courtesy of Land O'Lakes, Inc. Used with permission.

PAGE 106 Cherry Marketing Institute: Photo and recipe for Cherry-Chocolate Heart courtesy of The Cherry Marketing Institute. Used with permission.

PAGE 107 Kraft Foods: Recipe for Easter Bonnet Cake courtesy of Kraft Kitchens. Used with permission.

PAGE 108 Domino: Recipe for Banana Chiffon Cake courtesy of Domino Sugar. Used with permission.

PAGE 109 Sargento: Photo and recipe for Red, White & Blue Cheesecake courtesy of Sargento Foods Inc. Used with permission.

PAGE 110 Hershey: Recipe for Star Spangled Cocoa Bundt courtesy of Hershey Kitchens, Hershey Foods Corporation, Hershey, PA. Used with permission.

PAGE 111 Tone Brothers: Recipe for Flag Cookie Cake courtesy of Tone Brothers, Inc., producer of Tone's, Spice Islands, and Durkee products. Used with permission.

PAGE 112 Domino: Recipe for Chocolate Touchdown Cake courtesy of Domino Sugar. Used with permission.

PAGE 113 Sunkist: Recipe for Fresh Lemon Meringue Pie courtesy of Sunkist Growers, Inc. Used with permission.

PAGES 114/115 National Honey Board: Photo and recipe for Honey Passover Cheesecake courtesy of the National Honey Board. Used with permission.

PAGE 116 National Honey Board: Recipe for Honey Chiffon Cake courtesy of the National Honey Board. Used with permission.

PAGE 117 Hershey: Recipe for Pumpkin Faces courtesy of Hershey Kitchens, Hershey Foods Corporation, Hershey, PA. Used with permission.

PAGE 118 Domino: Recipe for Boo the Friendly Ghost Cake courtesy of Domino Sugar. Used with permission.

PAGE 119 Wisconsin Milk Marketing Board: Recipe for Holiday Date Cake courtesy of the Wisconsin Milk Marketing Board, Inc. Used with permission.

PAGE 120 American Egg Board: Photo and recipe for Plantation Pound Cake courtesy of the American Egg Board. Used with permission.

PAGE 121 American Egg Board: Recipe for Merry Meringue Cake courtesy of the American Egg Board. Used with permission.

PAGES 122/123 Hershey: Photo and recipe for Chocolate Cherry Valentine courtesy of Hershey Kitchens, Hershey Foods, Hershey, PA. Used with permission.

PAGE 124 Nestlé: Photo for Favorite Chocolate Cake courtesy of Nestlé. All trademarks are owned by Société des Produits Nestlé S.A., Vevey, Switzerland. Used with permission.

PAGES 126/127 Nestlé: Photo and recipe for Apple Cinnamon Pecan Cake courtesy of Nestlé. All trademarks are owned by Société des Produits Nestlé S.A., Vevey, Switzerland. Used with permission.

PAGE 128 Nestlé: Recipe for Favorite Chocolate Cake courtesy of Nestlé. All trademarks are owned by Société des Produits Nestlé S.A., Vevey, Switzerland. Used with permission.

PAGE 129 California Walnut Marketing Board: Photo and recipe for Maple Walnut Pound Cake courtesy of the California Walnut Marketing Board. Used with permission.

PAGE 130 Almond Board of California: Recipe for Mile High Almond Cake courtesy of the Almond Board of California. Used with permission.

PAGE 131 M&M/Mars: Recipe for Patriot Cake courtesy of M&M's® Brand Milk or Peanut Chocolate Candies. Used with permission.

PAGES 132/133 Land O'Lakes: Photo and recipe for 1-2-3-4 Butter Cake courtesy of Land O'Lakes, Inc. Used with permission.

PAGE 134 American Egg Board: Recipe for Orange Rum Savarin courtesy of the American Egg Board. Used with permission.

PAGE 135 National Honey Board: Recipe for Orange Honey Sponge Cake courtesy of the National Honey Board. Used with permission.

PAGE 136 McCormick: Recipe for Lemon Poppyseed Cake courtesy of McCormick. Used with permission.

PAGE 137 Dole: Photo and recipe for Banana Jewel Cake courtesy of Dole Food Company. Used with permission.

PAGES 138/139 Hershey: Photo and recipe for Take-Me-to-a-Picnic Cake courtesy of Hershey Kitchens, Hershey Foods, Hershey, PA. Used with permission.

# WEB SITES

**RODALE INC.**
www.rodale.com

Almond Board of California
www.almondsarein.com

American Egg Board
www.aeb.org

Bird's Eye Foods
www.birdseyefoods.com

© California Strawberry Commission
www.calstrawberry.com

California Walnut Marketing Board
www.walnuts.org

The Cherry Marketing Institute
www.usacherries.com

Del Monte Foods
www.delmonte.com

Dole Food Company
www.dole.com

Domino Sugar
www.dominosugar.com

Haagen-Dazs
www.haagen-dazs.com

Hershey
www.hersheykitchens.com

Kraft Foods
www.kraftfoods.com

Land O'Lakes, Inc.
www.landolakes.com

McCormick
www.mccormick.com

M&M's/Mars
www.marsbrightideas.com

National Honey Board
www.honey.com

Nestlé
www.verybestbaking.com

Ocean Spray Cranberries, Inc.
www.oceanspray.com

Sargento Foods Inc.
www.sargentocheese.com

Sugar in the Raw
www.sugarintheraw.com

Sunkist Growers, Inc.
www.sunkist.com

Tone Brothers, Inc.
www.spiceadvice.com

Wisconsin Milk Marketing Board, Inc.
www.wisdairy.com

# INDEX

✓ Designates a SuperQuick recipe that gets you in and out of the kitchen in 30 minutes or less!
**Boldface** page numbers refer to photographs. *Italicized* page numbers refer to boxed text.

ALMOND OIL
  Almond Glaze, 130
  Mile-High Almond Cake, 130
ALMONDS
  Almond Crunch Snack Cake, 38
  Almond & Mixed Berry Tart, 91
  Chocolate Almond Coffee Cake, 39, **39**
  ✓ Honey-Almond Sweet Pizza, 74
APPLE FRUIT FILLING
  Apple Cinnamon Cake, 26
  ✓ Quick & Easy Fruit Cobbler, 34
APPLE PIE FILLING
  Rustic Cranberry Apple Tart, 95, **95**
APPLES
  Apple Cinnamon Pecan Cake, 126, **127**
  Apple Colby Crisp, 36, **36**
  Blue Ribbon Apple Pie, **8**, 92
  for cobblers, *34*
  Dried Cherry Apple Pie, 89, **89**

BAKING SODA, *110*
BANANAS
  Banana Chiffon Cake, 108
  Banana Jewel Cake, 137, **137**
  Banana Tarts, 31
  Chocolate Banana Cream Pie, 52
  Extreme Banana Cream Pie, 32
BERRIES
  Almond & Mixed Berry Tart, 91
  for cobblers, *34*
  for crisps, *37*
BLUEBERRIES
  Fresh Blueberry Pie, 88
  Fresh Peach & Blueberry Pie, 87
BROWNIES. *See also* BROWNIES, NOVELTY FOR CHILDREN
  Chocolate Volcano, 48, **48**
BROWNIES, NOVELTY FOR CHILDREN. *See also* BROWNIES
  Graveyard Pizza, 73
  Jack O' Lantern, 71
  Winter Wonderland Snowmen, 77, **77**

CAKES. *See also* CHEESECAKES; COFFEE CAKES; CUPCAKES
  Apple Cinnamon Pecan Cake, 126, **127**
  Birthday Cake, 104, **105**
  Cinnamon Raisin Cake, **16**, 25
  cutting, *126*
  decorating, *12*
  determining when done, *45*
  Fabulous Carrot Cake, 24
  Flag Cookie Cake, 111
  frosting tips, 10–12, *105*, **105**, *123*
  Holiday Date Cake, 119
  keeping fresh, *30*
  Lemon Poppyseed Cake, 136
  Merry Meringue Cake, **102**, 121
  Mile-High Almond Cake, 130
  mixing, *10*
  Orange Rum Savarin, 134
  removing from pans, *71*
  splitting layers, *119*
CAKES, ANGEL FOOD
  Chocolate Angel Food Cake, 44
  decorating, *12*
  determining when done, *45*
  folding in egg whites, *108*
  keeping fresh, *30*
  mixing, *10*
  removing from pans, *71*
  salvaging collapsed, *44*
  tips for perfect, *44*
CAKES, BUNDT
  removing from pans, *71*
  Star Spangled Cocoa Bundt, 110
CAKES, BUTTER
  determining when done, *45*
  keeping fresh, *30*
  1-2-3-4 Butter Cake, **2**, 132, **133**
  troubleshooting tips, *133*
CAKES, CAKE-MIX BASED
  Apple Cinnamon Cake, 26
  Banana Jewel Cake, 137, **137**
  Black Forest Cake, 59
  Bunny Cake, 75, **75**
  Butterfly Cake, 69
  Candy 'n' Balloon Birthday Cake, **64,** 70
  Cherry-Mallow Cake, 23, **23**
  Choco-holic Cake, **10, 40,** 43
  Chocolate Angel Food Cake, 44
  Dinosaur Birthday Cake, 72, **72**
  Easter Bonnet Cake, 107
  Holiday Eggnog Cake, 100
  Midnight Bliss Cake, 45
  Patriot Cake, 131
  Peanutty Goober Cake, 78, **78**
  Pumpkin Spice Cake, 98
  Sand Castle Cake, 68
CAKES, CHIFFON
  Banana Chiffon Cake, 108
  decorating, *12*
  determining when done, *45*
  folding in egg whites, *108*
  Honey Chiffon Cake, 116
  keeping fresh, *30*
  mixing, *10*
  removing from pans, *71*
CAKES, CHOCOLATE
  Black Forest Cake, 59
  Boo the Friendly Ghost Cake, 118
  Choco-holic Cake, **10, 40,** 43
  Chocolate Angel Food Cake, 44
  Chocolate Cherry Valentine, **15**, 122–23, **123**
  Chocolate Espresso Fudge Cake, 63
  Chocolate Touchdown Cake, 112
  Easy Fudge Cake with Buttercream Frosting, 58
  Favorite Chocolate Cake, **124,** 128
  Heritage Chocolate Cake, 60, **61**
  Midnight Bliss Cake, 45
  Mile-High Chocolate Cake, 46, **47**
  Red Velvet Cake, 42, 43
  Special Dark Picnic Cake, 62
  Star Spangled Cocoa Bundt, 110
  Take-Me-to-a-Picnic Cake, 138, **139**
  3-Layer German Sweet Chocolate Cake, 49
CAKES, FOAM
  decorating, *12*
  determining when done, *45*
  folding in egg whites, *108*
  glazing, *12*
  keeping fresh, *30*
  mixing, *10*
  removing from pans, *71*

CAKES, ICE CREAM
  Black-Out Cake, *11*
  constructing, *11*
  Frozen Key Lime Torte, 97
  Ice Cream Cake Roll, **10**, 27, **27**
  Maple-Nut Cake, *11*
  Peach Melba Cake, *11*
CAKES, LAYER
  frosting, *11*, *105*, **105**, *123*
  mixing, *10*
  removing from pans, *71*
  splitting fast, *119*
CAKES, NOVELTY FOR CHILDREN
  Boo the Friendly Ghost Cake, 118
  Brownie Mud Puddle Cake, 66–67, **67**
  Bunny Cake, 75, **75**
  Butterfly Cake, 69
  Candy 'n' Balloon Birthday Cake, **64,** 70
  Chocolate Chip Cookie Cake, 76
  decorating, *73*
  Dinosaur Birthday Cake, 72, **72**
  Flag Cookie Cake, 111
  Patriot Cake, 131
  Peanutty Goober Cake, 78, **78**
  Sand Castle Cake, 68
CAKES, POUND
  Buttery Pound Cake, 22, **22**
  Holiday Fruited Pound Cake, **82,** 101
  Maple Walnut Pound Cake, 129, **129**
  Plantation Pound Cake, 120, **120**
CAKES, POUND (FROZEN)
  as ice cream cake base, *11*
CAKES, PUDDING
  Choco-holic Cake, **10, 40,** 43
  Midnight Bliss Cake, 45
  Pumpkin Spice Cake, 98
CAKES, SPONGE
  decorating, *12*
  determining when done, *45*
  folding in egg whites, *108*
  keeping fresh, *30*
  mixing, *10*
  Orange Honey Sponge Cake, 135
  removing from pans, *71*
CAKES, UPSIDE-DOWN
  designing, *12*
  Peach Upside-Down Cake, 29
  Pineapple Upside-Down Cake, **28**, 29
CARROTS
  Fabulous Carrot Cake, 24
CHEESE, COLBY
  Apple Colby Crisp, 36, **36**
CHEESECAKES
  Cranberry Pumpkin Cheesecake, 99, **99**
  Dark Chocolate Layered Cheesecake, 57
  Honey Passover Cheesecake, 114, **115**
  keeping fresh, *30*
  Red, White & Blue Cheesecake, 109, **109**
  'Tis Spring! Cheesecake, 84
  Triple Chocolate Cheesecake, **15**, 50
CHEESECAKES, CRUSTS FOR
  Chocolate Crumb Crust, 57
  Matzo Meal Tart Shell, 114, **115**
  for Red, White & Blue Cheesecake, 109, **109**
  for Triple Chocolate Cheesecake, 50

142  BLUE RIBBON CAKES & PIES

CHERRIES
  crisps of, 37
  Dried Cherry Apple Pie, 89, **89**
  Holiday Eggnog Cake, 100
CHERRY PIE FILLING
  Black Forest Cake, 59
  Cherry-Chocolate Heart, 106, **106**
  Cherry-Mallow Cake, 23, **23**
  Chocolate Cherry Valentine, **15**, 122–23, **123**
CHILDREN
  treats for (*See* Brownies, novelty for children; Cakes, novelty for children)
CHOCOLATE
  melting, 52
  preventing liquefying in pies, 51
CHOCOLATE DESSERTS. *SEE ALSO* BROWNIES
  Black-Out Cake, 11
  Cherry-Chocolate Heart, 106, **106**
  Chocolate Almond Coffee Cake, 39, **39**
  Chocolate Volcano, 48, **48**
  Pumpkin Faces, **15**, 117
CHOCOLATE DESSERTS, CAKES
  Black Forest Cake, 59
  Boo the Friendly Ghost Cake, 118
  Brownie Mud Puddle Cake, 66–67, **67**
  Choco-holic Cake, **10, 40,** 43
  Chocolate Angel Food Cake, 44
  Chocolate Cherry Valentine, **15**, 122–23, **123**
  Chocolate Chip Cookie Cake, 76
  Chocolate Espresso Fudge Cake, 63
  Chocolate Touchdown Cake, 112
  Easy Fudge Cake with Buttercream Frosting, 58
  Favorite Chocolate Cake, **124,** 128
  Heritage Chocolate Cake, 60, **61**
  Midnight Bliss Cake, 45
  Mile-High Chocolate Cake, 46, **47**
  Peanutty Goober Cake, 78, **78**
  Red Velvet Cake, 42
  Special Dark Picnic Cake, 62
  Star Spangled Cocoa Bundt, 110
  Take-Me-to-a-Picnic Cake, 138, **139**
  3-Layer German Sweet Chocolate Cake, 49
CHOCOLATE DESSERTS, CHEESECAKES
  Dark Chocolate Layered Cheesecake, 57
  Triple Chocolate Cheesecake, **15**, 50
CHOCOLATE DESSERTS, PIES
  Brownie Bottom Pudding Pie, **13**, 53, **53**
  Chocolate Banana Cream Pie, 52
  Chocolate Pecan Pie, 56
  Gone to Heaven Chocolate Pie, **10**, 51
  White Chocolate Coconut Cream Pie, **54,** 55
COBBLERS
  fruits for, 34
  Quick & Easy Fruit Cobbler, 34
  Simply Good Cobbler, 35, **35**
COCONUT
  Coconut-Pecan Filling & Frosting, 49
  Toasted Coconut Crumb, 14
  White Chocolate Coconut Cream Pie, **54,** 55
COFFEE CAKES
  Almond Crunch Snack Cake, 38
  Chocolate Almond Coffee Cake, 39, **39**

COOKIES
  S'more Cookie Bars, 74
CRANBERRIES
  Cranberry Pecan Pie, 94
  freezing, 48
  Rustic Cranberry Apple Tart, 95, **95**
CRANBERRY SAUCE
  Cranberry Pumpkin Cheesecake, 99, **99**
CREAM, HEAVY. *SEE ALSO* CREAM, WHIPPED
  Vanilla Cream Filling, 123
  whipping ultra-pasteurized, 14–15
CREAM, WHIPPED. *SEE ALSO* CREAM, HEAVY
  Chocolate Whipped Cream, **15,** 123, **123**
  Honey Whipped Cream, 135
  Orange Whipped Cram, 90
  stabilizing, 15
  Vanilla Whipped Cream, 63
  whipping tips for, 14–15
CRISPS
  Apple Colby Crisp, 36, **36**
  berry, 37
  cherry, 37
  Easy Peach Crisp, 37
  nectarine, 37
  pear, 37
  plum, 37
CRUSTS, CRUMB
  Chocolate Crumb Crust, 57
  Cinnamony Graham Crust, 14
  No-Bake Southern Pecan Crust, 14
  for Red, White & Blue Cheesecake, 109, **109**
  Snappy Ginger Crust, 14
  Toasted Coconut Crumb, 14
  for Triple Chocolate Cheesecake, 50
CRUSTS, FOR CHEESECAKES
  Matzo Meal Tart Shell, 114, **115**
  for Red, White & Blue Cheesecake, 109, **109**
  for Triple Chocolate Cheesecake, 50
CRUSTS, FOR PIES AND TARTS
  for Almond & Mixed Berry Tart, 91
  for Blue Ribbon Apple Pie, **8,** 92
  Cinnamony Graham Crust, 14
  for cream pies, 12
  creating fancy edges, 94, **94**
  creating flaky, 12
  creating lattice tops, 88, **88**
  creating tender, 12
  for Lemon Ribbon Ice Cream Pie, 96
  No-Bake Southern Pecan Crust, 14
  pre-baking, 12
  preventing soggy, 12
  rolling out, 33
  Snappy Ginger Crust, 14
  Toasted Coconut Crumb, 14
  transferring, 33, **33**
CUPCAKES. *SEE ALSO* CAKES
  converting cake recipes to, 81
CUPCAKES, CAKE-MIX BASED
  Cupid's Cupcakes, **80,** 81
  Dalmatian Cupcakes, 79, **79**
  Easter Bonnet Cake, 107
  Light Spice Cupcakes, 30
CUPCAKES, NOVELTY FOR CHILDREN
  Cupid's Cupcakes, **80,** 81
  Dalmatian Cupcakes, 79, **79**
  Easter Bonnet Cake, 107
  Pumpkin Faces, **15,** 117

DATES
  Holiday Date Cake, 119
EGGNOG
  Holiday Eggnog Cake, 100
EGGS
  folding in egg whites, 108
  tempering yolks, 32
ESPRESSO
  Chocolate Espresso Fudge Cake, 63
FILLINGS
  Coconut-Pecan Filling & Frosting, 49
  Vanilla Cream Filling, 123
FOOD FACTS
  birthday cakes, history of, 69
  Black Forest Cake history, 59
FROSTINGS. *SEE ALSO* GLAZES
  Birthday Frosting, 104, **105**
  for Candy 'n' Balloon Birthday Cake, **64,** 70
  Chocolate Buttercream Frosting, 112
  Chocolate Butter Frosting, **2,** 132, **133**
  Chocolate Fudge Frosting, 60, **61**
  Chocolate Whipped Cream, **15,** 123, **123**
  Coconut-Pecan Filling & Frosting, 49
  Cream Cheese Frosting, 98
  Dark Frosting, 62
  Decorator's Icing, 112
  for Fabulous Carrot Cake, 24
  Fluffy Buttercream Frosting, 42, 58
  Frosting for the Pumpkins, **15,** 117
  Lemony Cream Cheese Frosting, 24
  Peanut Butter Chip Frosting, 138, **139**
  Pink Frost Icing, **80,** 81
  Seven Minute Frosting, 118
  techniques for, 10–12, **105, 105,** 123
FROZEN DESSERTS. *SEE* CAKES, ICE CREAM; ICE CREAM DESSERTS
FRUIT DESSERTS. *SEE* SPECIFIC FRUIT
FRUIT, MIXED
  Simply Good Cobbler, 35, **35**

GARNISHES
  for children's cakes, 73
  Chocolate Garnish, 139, **139**
  Easy Marshmallow Snails, 66–67, **67**
GELATIN-BASED DESSERTS
  Easy Marshmallow Snails, 66–67, **67**
GINGERSNAPS
  Snappy Ginger Crust, 14
GLAZES. *SEE ALSO* FROSTINGS
  Almond Glaze, 130
  Caramel Glaze, **16,** 25
  for Chocolate Chip Cookie Cake, 76
  Chocolate Glaze, 39, **39**
  for Holiday Eggnog Cake, 100
  for Ice Cream Cake Roll, **10,** 27, **27**
  Jelly Glaze, 112
  Lemon Glaze, 136
  Maple Glaze, 129, **129**
  Rum Glaze, **82,** 101
GRAHAM CRACKERS
  Cinnamony Graham Crust, 14
GRAPEFRUIT
  Citrus Mini Tarts, 90

HONEY
  ✓Honey-Almond Sweet Pizza, 74
  Honey Chiffon Cake, 116
  Honey Passover Cheesecake, 114, **115**
  Honey-Pecan Topping, 94
  Honey Whipped Cream, 135
  Orange Honey Sponge Cake, 135

ICE CREAM DESSERTS
  Black-Out Cake, *11*
  constructing cakes, *11*
  Frozen Key Lime Torte, 97
  Ice Cream Cake Roll, **10**, **27**, *27*
  Lemon Ribbon Ice Cream Pie, 96
  Maple-Nut Cake, *11*
  Peach Melba Cake, *11*

LEMON JUICE
  Fresh Lemon Meringue Pie, 113
  Lemon Ribbon Ice Cream Pie, 96
LEMON PEEL
  Lemon Poppyseed Cake, 136
LEMON ZEST
  Fresh Lemon Meringue Pie, 113
  Lemon Ribbon Ice Cream Pie, 96
LIME JUICE
  Frozen Key Lime Torte, 97

MACE, 30
MARSHMALLOWS
  Cherry-Mallow Cake, 23, **23**
  Easy Marshmallow Snails, 66–67, **67**
MATZO MEAL
  Matzo Meal Tart Shell, 114, **115**
MENUS
  for backyard barbecue, 87
  for spring brunch, 26
MERINGUE
  preventing weeping, *121*
  Three-Egg Meringue, 113
MILK
  souring, 110

NECTARINES
  crisps of, 37

ORANGE JUICE
  ✓Citrus Mini Tarts, 90
  Orange Honey Sponge Cake, 135
  Orange Rum Savarin, 134
  Orange Whipped Cream, 90
ORANGE PEEL
  Orange Honey Sponge Cake, 135
ORANGE ZEST
  Orange Whipped Cream, 90
ORANGES
  ✓Citrus Mini Tarts, 90

PASTRY. SEE CRUSTS, FOR PIES AND TARTS
PEACHES
  Berry Sour Cream Shortcake, 20, **21**
  ✓Easy Peach Crisp, 37
  Fresh Peach & Blueberry Pie, 87
  Peach Upside-Down Cake, 29
PEACH FRUIT FILLING
  Apple Cinnamon Cake, 26
  ✓Quick & Easy Fruit Cobbler, 34
PEANUT BUTTER
  Peanutty Goober Cake, 78, **78**

PEANUT BUTTER CHIPS
  Peanut Butter Chip Frosting, 138, **139**
PEARS
  crisps of, 37
PECANS
  Apple Cinnamon Pecan Cake, 126, **127**
  Chocolate Pecan Pie, 56
  Classic Southern Pecan Pie, 33
  Coconut-Pecan Filling & Frosting, 49
  Cranberry Pecan Pie, 94
  Honey-Pecan Topping, 94
  No-Bake Southern Pecan Crust, 14
PIE CRUSTS. SEE CRUSTS, FOR PIES AND TARTS
PIES. SEE ALSO TARTS
  Blue Ribbon Apple Pie, **8**, 92
  Classic Southern Pecan Pie, 33
  Cranberry Pecan Pie, 94
  Dried Cherry Apple Pie, 89, **89**
  Famous Pumpkin Pie, 93, **93**
  Fresh Blueberry Pie, 88
  Fresh Lemon Meringue Pie, 113
  Fresh Peach & Blueberry Pie, 87
  speed baking apple, *12*
  Strawberry Rhubarb Custard Pie, 86, **86**
PIES, CHOCOLATE
  Brownie Bottom Pudding Pie, **13**, 53, **53**
  Chocolate Banana Cream Pie, 52
  Chocolate Pecan Pie, 56
  Gone to Heaven Chocolate Pie, **10**, 51
  preventing liquefied, *51*
PIES, CREAM
  Chocolate Banana Cream Pie, 52
  crusts for, *12*
  Extreme Banana Cream Pie, 32
  tips for making, *32*
  White Chocolate Coconut Cream Pie, **54**, 55
PIES, ICE CREAM
  Lemon Ribbon Ice Cream Pie, 96
PINEAPPLE
  Pineapple Upside-Down Cake, **28**, 29
PIZZA, DESSERT
  Graveyard Pizza, 73
  ✓Honey-Almond Sweet Pizza, 74
PLUMS
  crisps of, 37
PUDDING-BASED DESSERTS
  Brownie Bottom Pudding Pie, **13**, 53, **53**
  Brownie Mud Puddle Cake, 66–67, **67**
  Choco-holic Cake, **10**, **40**, 43
  Chocolate Banana Cream Pie, 52
  Extreme Banana Cream Pie, 32
  Midnight Bliss Cake, 45
  White Chocolate Coconut Cream Pie, **54**, 55
PUMMELOS (POMELO, POMMELO)
  ✓Citrus Mini Tarts, 90
PUMPKIN
  Cranberry Pumpkin Cheesecake, 99, **99**
  Famous Pumpkin Pie, 93, **93**
  Pumpkin Spice Cake, 98

RAISINS
  Cinnamon Raisin Cake, **16**, 25
  Holiday Eggnog Cake, 100
RASPBERRIES
  Berry Sour Cream Shortcake, 20, **21**

SAUCES, DESSERT
  Raspberry Sauce, 63
SAVARINS. SEE CAKES
SHORTCAKES
  Berry Sour Cream Shortcake, 20, **21**
  Classic Strawberry Shortcake, 18
  key to perfect, *18*
  Strawberry Angel Shortcakes, 19
S'MORES
  S'more Cookie Bars, 74
STRAWBERRIES
  Classic Strawberry Shortcake, 18
  Strawberry Angel Shortcakes, 19
  Strawberry Crown Tart, 85, **85**
  Strawberry Rhubarb Custard Pie, 86, **86**

TARTS. SEE ALSO PIES
  Almond & Mixed Berry Tart, 91
  Banana Tarts, 31
  ✓Citrus Mini Tarts, 90
  Rustic Cranberry Apple Tart, 95, **95**
  Strawberry Crown Tart, 85, **85**
TECHNIQUES
  chocolate, melting, *52*
  chocolate, preventing liquefying, *51*
  egg yolks, tempering, *32*
  ice cream cakes, constructing, *11*
  meringue, preventing weeping, *121*
  sour milk, making, *110*
  whipping cream, *14–15*
TECHNIQUES, CAKES
  angel food tips, *44*
  butter cake troubleshooting, *133*
  cutting, *126*
  decorating, *12*
  determining when done, *45*
  folding in egg whites, *108*
  frosting tips, *10–12*, **105**, *105*, *123*
  keeping fresh, *30*
  mixing, *10*
  removing from pans, *71*
  splitting layers, *119*
TECHNIQUES, PIES
  cream pie tips, *32*
  creating flaky crusts, *12*
  creating tender crusts, *12*
  fancy edges for crusts, 94, **94**
  lattice tops, creating, 88, **88**
  pre-baking crusts, *12*
  preventng soggy crusts, *12*
  rolling out crusts, *33*
  transferring crusts, *33*, **33**
TOPPINGS, DESSERT
  crumb for Fresh Peach & Blueberry Pie, 87
  Crunch Topping, 38
  Honey-Pecan Topping, 94
  Honey Whipped Cream, 135
  Streusel Topping, 39, **39**
  Three-Egg Meringue, 113
TORTES, FROZEN
  Frozen Key Lime Torte, 97

VANILLA WAFERS
  No-Bake Southern Pecan Crust, 14

WALNUTS
  Maple Walnut Pound Cake, 129, **129**
WHIPPED CREAM. SEE CREAM, WHIPPED